WAR FRONTS
HOME FIRES

Joseph W. McQuaid

War Fronts – Home Fires
Copyright © 2023 Joseph W. McQuaid

Cover design and digital formatting: The Killion Group, Inc.

DEDICATION

For my family.
In memory of B.J. and Peg McQuaid.

FOREWORD

DURING WORLD WAR II, newspaper friends and family members told B.J. McQuaid that they expected he would write a book about his experiences, as several other war correspondents had already done. He had plenty of material, having covered three fronts of the war in almost four years. His articles, often with his name in the headline, were featured in American newspapers as well as in colleagues' books and articles.

He mentioned the book in letters to his wife, but it never happened. Whether he was too busy reuniting with and expanding his family, starting a newspaper, dealing with diabetes and other health issues, or just wanting to forget much of what he had seen, he didn't write a book — until now.

In many ways, this is my father's book. He wrote much of it through his news stories and letters to my mother, from which I quote at length.
I hope he likes it.

———∽∽∽———

Cover Photo:
Home for Christmas after two years at the front, with another
18 months looming, B.J. and Peg McQuaid show daughter
Judy and son John where he has traveled.

A FEW NOTES TO THE READER

M Y MOTHER, MARGARET Griffin McQuaid, was almost always called "Peg" or sometimes "Peggy" by friends and family. My father, Bernard John McQuaid, was "Bernie" to his family, "Barney" to his wartime colleagues, and B.J. McQuaid for his byline. For consistency, I refer to them as Peg and B.J. throughout this book.

During World War II, the term "Jap" was widely used to describe Japanese persons in a derogatory way that is unthinkable today. It appeared in the headlines of major newspapers, as well as in radio broadcasts and film newsreels, books, and magazines. I understand its use may make readers uncomfortable, and I only include it here when it is part of a direct quote.

My parents' letters, and my father's drafts and published articles are included unedited, except for a few minor changes made for clarity. While many of his stories appear throughout this work, additional pieces are added at the end of most chapters.

AMERICA IN THE WAR

Well before Japan's surprise attack on the U.S. Navy's Pacific Fleet at Pearl Harbor, Hawaii, on December 7, 1941, B.J., Peg, and their friends were aware of the war already raging in Europe and the Pacific. In the mid-1930s, Fascists in Germany, Italy, and Spain had seized power; the Empire of Japan was brutalizing the Chinese.

Colonel Frank Knox, who owned the Chicago Daily News and also the New Hampshire newspapers where B.J. (and Peg, briefly) had worked, was named Secretary of the Navy in 1940 by President Franklin Delano Roosevelt. Both men knew that America could not avoid this new war for much longer. They would need to prepare the nation.

"Whatever the U.S. stake in foreign matters, Americans were beginning to see and hear the world through their newspapers, which traditionally had given much more coverage to Main Street than to global affairs, and from their radios...Newspapers had awakened with the diplomats when the Munich Pact was signed. Sensing the importance of the pact, the Associated Press covered the events as a major news story...." So explained authors Norman Polmar and Thomas B. Allen in their book, World War II: America at War 1941-1945.

In September 1938, Adolf Hitler bullied France and England into signing the Munich Agreement allowing Germany to take control of parts of Czechoslovakia. He then signed a non-aggression pact with Soviet Union boss Josef Stalin, ignoring the "Peace in Our Time" idea that the United Kingdom's Prime Minister Neville Chamberlain claimed would ensue as the result of the Munich Agreement. Germany's *Blitzkrieg*, or "lightning war," soon rolled over Poland with Soviet assistance.

Next to fall was France, in the spring of 1940, leaving a flotilla of small British civilian boats to rescue thousands of soldiers from Dunkirk, France. The British were left alone in Europe to confront Hitler. They rallied 'round the new U.K. Prime Minister, Winston Churchill, as their war leader.

The air Battle of Britain followed, from July to October 1940, with many Americans cheering for the Brits but even more insisting that the U.S. fight no more foreign wars. Famed aviator Charles Lindbergh was a leader of the isolationist America First Committee, a nationwide organization opposing U.S. intervention in the war. An equally isolationist Congress passed measures severely restricting American aid to foreign countries. Furthermore, our own military was small and in a sad state.

The anti-war sentiment prevailed until the surprise attack on Pearl Harbor. The U.S. declared war on Japan the next day, December 8, 1941. Hitler and Italy's Mussolini quickly declared war on America. Soviet strongman Stalin's pact with Germany lasted until Hitler ignored that, too, and invaded the Soviet Union in June 1941. Stalin then joined with the Allies.

In some ways, World War II was a continuation of World War I, where the victors (the United Kingdom, the United States, and France) punished the losers (primarily Germany) with onerous war reparations and severe military restrictions. Japan was also hungry for more territory and felt fenced in by the United States cutting its oil supplies.

The U.S. entry into the war changed its course, although it took time. America ramped up military production, instituted a draft, and contended with both a Pacific war against Japan, and a European and Mideast one against Hitler and Mussolini. The Aleutian Islands, part of Alaska and B.J. McQuaid's first war front, were invaded by the Japanese as part of a wider Pacific plan to thwart the United States. President Roosevelt had to let the Pacific fronts take second spot while he dealt with Europe. Even so, the U.S. Navy and U.S. Marine Corps engaged with Japan and drove its forces steadily back toward its homeland.

The European campaign began with the Allies confronting Germany in North Africa and then in the Mediterranean and Italy before amassing strength in England for the D-Day assault on Normandy, France, on June 6, 1944.

The Americans and British, under the overall command of U.S. General Dwight D. Eisenhower, fought across Europe from the West while the Soviets did so from the East, ultimately ending in Germany's collapse and Hitler's suicide in April 1945.

What B.J. witnessed and reported on during World War II was by no means a complete picture. The war consumed and affected much of the world and millions of people. No one person could see it all. But B.J. McQuaid saw an awful lot of it.

More than 80 years later, I believe his work and his frontline reporting still add texture and context to the war's history. Along with his letters to his wife and hers to him, they provided me with a better understanding of that tumultuous time and a deeper appreciation of the people who faced it and survived. I hope it does the same for others.

INTRODUCTION

The personal request was added at the end of a 1,000-word story datelined "December twenty fifth with American forces in Ardennes."

It was 1944, and readers in the United States may have gone to their maps of Europe, often printed in their newspapers, to search for that location. It would soon become famous as the site of the Battle of the Bulge, Adolf Hitler's last desperate attempt to turn the tide of a war that he had started but would not live to finish.

The Germans' daring surprise attack targeted an area in the Allies' lines that was undermanned and held in part by relatively new American troops. Having roared across France during that summer and fall with dazzling speed, the Allies were on the verge of crossing into Germany itself.

But on Christmas Day, the war's outcome was suddenly in doubt. Fighting was fierce along what the brass called a "fluid" front. Elements of the 101st Airborne Division were surrounded at Bastogne, Belgium. Three days earlier, an American commander's response to a German demand for surrender was just one word: "Nuts!"

Bernard J. McQuaid, a war correspondent for the highly regarded Chicago Daily News Foreign Service (CDN), had not been heard from for several days. He was going out to assess the situation for himself, he had told his editor, and he expected to be out of contact for a while.

His note was brief:

"Service message Mariano. Please send Love Christmas greetings [to] my wife family via Western Union to Manchester New Hampshire Stop Tell them this heartfelt though belated by fact eye [sic] spent last three days in combat areas."

"Greetings to you too," he added, addressing Tony Mariano, the CDN New York City transmission overseer who had processed hundreds of his stories.

McQuaid's news story that day was typical of many of his pieces. He was in the middle of the action, trying to make sense of the situation and reporting on individual soldiers as well as their commanders.

Other than a brief break at Christmastime one year earlier, B.J. had been away from his home, his wife, and his two young children for nearly three years. He had missed birthdays and holidays, weddings, funerals, and every-days, as he reported from the American and British front lines of World War II.

He began his war reporting in the frozen Aleutian Islands off Alaska in 1942. He then spent much of 1943 covering sea battles and island combat in the sweltering South Pacific where he contracted malaria and aggravated painful skin diseases that would remain with him for much of his life. Now it was Christmas Day, 1944, and B.J. had been covering the war in Europe since the June 6 D-Day landings at Normandy. It would be another half a year before he came home for good.

McQuaid's stories were of big battles and small details. He saw the sacrifices and smelled the stench of death as U.S. Marines fought to wrest Tarawa, an obscure Pacific atoll, from the Japanese. Landing on Utah Beach on D-Day Plus One, he saw sailors blown into the air as a boat next to him struck a landmine.

During that summer of 1944, he followed General George S. Patton's dash across France. He also confronted Patton himself in defense of a press officer in trouble for briefing correspondents about a top-secret operation.

One night he and a fellow correspondent slept in an eerily dark and quiet hotel outside of Paris just before that city's liberation, discovering later that German soldiers were also sleeping there that night.

B.J. narrowly avoided death several times and missed being taken prisoner on one occasion only because he stopped to ask for directions. He was in the Netherlands as British Field Marshal Bernard Law Montgomery oversaw the disastrous Operation Market Garden. He also saw a Nazi death camp there and wrote of Dutch civilians trying to hide Jews from the Nazi Holocaust, which was by then no secret to his readers.

McQuaid's stories were featured in more than 80 newspapers large and small, across the United States and Canada, as well as in Britain and Australia. The Chicago Daily News Service was considered by many editors to be the best American news service reporting worldwide. Its total circulation was nearly 10 million, with readership considerably higher in an era when families shared and sometimes fought over the newspaper. The CDN was a major source of news, foreign and domestic. Several radio stations also subscribed to it.

During the war and for years thereafter, McQuaid received letters from GIs or their families who clipped and saved his stories, which were often the only word they had for months or more about their sons, husbands, and fathers. Sometimes, as well, it was the only way his own family knew where he was.
Back in small-town New Hampshire, his wife, Peg, was keeping the home fires burning for herself and their two small children. It wasn't easy. It meant much more sacrifice than most Americans have gone through since.

It meant figuring out and filing government forms for the heating oil allotment that would keep them warm during New Hampshire's war winters, a few of which saw the temperature drop to 30 and 40 degrees below zero.

For Peg McQuaid, it also meant dealing with the rationing of food and gasoline. Even her shoe purchases were limited by the government. *Three pairs allowed per year,* she wrote to her husband, adding that she only needed one pair, so it wasn't a problem.

It meant learning to preserve fruits and vegetables to see them through the winter and searching widely for scarce items like butter and coffee. It also meant taking her turn as an air raid warden, even though the chances of enemy aircraft targeting tiny Candia, New Hampshire, seemed quite small.

B.J. retained some of Peg's war letters to him and copies of his to her, in a small trunk, which stayed largely undisturbed for decades in a hayloft in their Candia home. Peg wasn't a trained reporter like B.J., but she was well-read and highly intelligent and had attended a year at a women's junior college.

When I began writing this book, I wanted it to be simply about my father covering the war. I had read many of his published pieces, and when I was a boy, he would tell me other stories, always with his Lucky Strike cigarettes and Scotch whisky at hand—and often late into the night—in the Candia home to which he returned after the war.

He figured into others' war accounts, too. Celebrated <u>Time Life</u> correspondent Robert Sherrod quoted my father in his compelling book, <u>Tarawa: The Story of a Battle</u>. The acclaimed film director and screenwriter John Huston included one of McQuaid's stories in his autobiography, <u>An Open Book</u>. Other correspondents also wrote about some of B.J.'s adventures.

But this is also my mother's story and the story of two people deeply in love and, like millions of others, dealing with separation and challenge, heartache, fear, and hope. The things they experienced during the war are, in some ways, what life can throw at any of us, but not, I think, with such ferocity as it did for their generation. The experiences of World War II changed them forever.

Newsman and author Tom Brokaw famously called theirs America's "greatest generation." My father would dismiss that as "bullshit," but I think Brokaw had it right. These men and women were special, and their stories deserve to be told.

CHAPTER ONE

WHY HE'S GOING

B.J. at his Chicago Daily News desk, 1941.

EVEN AS HE prepared to cover the war on its front lines–from somewhere, anywhere–B.J. McQuaid wondered if he was doing the right thing. His family was living in Chicago, where their first son had been born, while he worked as an editorial writer and aviation reporter for the Chicago Daily News, owned by Col. Frank Knox.

In the late spring of 1942, B.J. moved Peg and their children, five-year-old Judy and Johnny, just 18 months old, back to New Hampshire, to his hometown of Candia, a rural community 12 miles east of Manchester, the small state's largest city.

They resumed residence in a modest Cape Cod-style house on South Road. It was a wedding gift from her father. Married in

1936, they lived there briefly before Col. Knox, who also owned the local papers (the <u>Manchester Union</u> and <u>Evening Leader</u>), brought them to the Windy City.

Winding things up in Chicago and about to leave for the West Coast and assignment overseas in June 1942, B.J. wrote to Peg back in Candia.

> *Did I detect in our phone conversation the other night some doubt or hesitancy on your part as to whether I ought to go ahead with this business of reporting the war?*

> *Frankly, I've had doubts, too. There are moments when I feel like calling all bets off, and slinking back to South Road. These moments will probably become more intense, and more frequent, as I get closer to the scene of activity. But you really don't want me to quit, Peg, and I hope I shan't be such poor, weak fish as that."*

B.J. wrote that he was following this course because *"I can't see any other which would permit me to look myself in the eye or–what's much more important–feel deserving of your good opinion."*

There were things, he conceded, of which he was not proud. He didn't specify them.

> *"But there are three or four fundamental things in which I would hate to consider myself deficient. This matter of fighting for your own country–which means ultimately your wife and kids and their chances of a decent break–is one of them.*

> *"It's true my weapon is only a typewriter, but that is quite a formidable weapon, as our enemies have shown [Hitler's propaganda machine was repeating the*

same lies, over and over, to great effect]. And I shall be employing them at the front–not from an office in Washington."

It may sound a little vainglorious, he continued, "but I was never in my life more sincere.

"And please believe that I realize you have a bigger and tougher job in this than I. If I didn't know you would do that job, faithfully and well, I couldn't go on for an instant. You're my home front, my source of supply and base of communications. Whatever courage and enterprise and will I'm able to put into the job comes straight from you. I'm sure you know that. You must know it. The children? I told you–I don't allow myself to think of the children. Everything else I can bear tolerably well, but that I can't bear."

He could have invented many excuses not to go, *but "you wouldn't believe them and I wouldn't.*

"The greatest thing there can be between a man and a woman–beyond love, and we have that–is mutual respect. I have much more respect for you–as an animal of high courage, honesty, and strength of more fiber–then you can possibly know.

"If I do a really good job at this business, and stand up well under fire (which God help me to do) it will add to your respect for me, and our very lives will be enriched by it, through the years to come.

B.J. told Peg he got a kick out of a friend's wife whose husband was about to join a combat unit *"going around demanding of all males under 40 why they aren't in the fight too."*

"Peg," he said, *"had done the same on occasion."*
"It's that sort of thing that gives a bozo a lift.

*"So long as you're standing up at home, rooting for
me, looking after the cubs, maintaining the home
base–how did the old song put it? 'Keep the home fires
burning.'*

"So long as you do that nothing will ever get me down.

B.J. ended the letter with a request that he would repeat many
times during the next three years and that his wife would try her
best to fulfill.

*"Write to me, darling. Long letters–full of everything
trivial and unimportant.*

*"Kiss Judy and Johnny for me. As for yourself–
oh, lamb, lamb, lamb–Don't ever stop loving and
praying."*
He signed it *B.*

At first, B.J. wasn't sure where he wanted to go to cover the
war. His Chicago editors seemed unsure of where to send him.
A keen student of aviation and a licensed pilot before the war,
he often wrote on the subject when he wasn't writing editorials.
Twice he did so from Canada, reporting on Canadian and
American air forces training there. Even before the Japanese
attack on Pearl Harbor brought the United States into the war,
B.J. asked Col. Knox about becoming a foreign correspondent
or enlisting in the armed forces.

Knox was both a mentor and father figure to B.J., whose own
father had nominally worked under Knox when the latter was
overseeing the newspapers of William Randolph Hearst. Elias
McQuaid died of a heart attack while working as an editorial
writer and political reporter for Hearst's <u>Boston American</u>
newsaper.

Among his colleagues and employees, Knox was known
simply as "the Colonel"—the rank to which he had risen while

serving as an artillery officer during World War I. Before that, he was one of the legendary Rough Riders in Leonard Wood's and Theodore Roosevelt's volunteer cavalry unit that fought in Cuba during the Spanish-American War.

The Knox-Roosevelt friendship endured, with Knox starting a Manchester newspaper (the Evening Leader) as he promoted Roosevelt's Bull Moose presidential run in 1912. Teddy lost that race, but Knox soon bought a competing paper, the Morning Union, where Elias McQuaid had also once worked.

Knox also ran for political office, losing the nomination as the Republican candidate for New Hampshire governor in 1924 to future U.S. Ambassador to the U.K. John Winant, and then as a GOP presidential contender. He lost the 1936 Republican nomination to Gov. Alf Landon of Kansas and then joined the ticket that was crushed in Franklin Delano Roosevelt's bid for a second term.

To the great distaste and dismay of many fellow Republicans, Knox accepted FDR's request to become Secretary of the Navy in 1940. With war clouds looming, FDR wanted to show a united and bipartisan front at home, where most people wanted nothing to do with Europe's troubles for a second time in 25 years.

In April 1941, Knox wrote to tell B.J. that he sympathized and appreciated his spirit, "but I still am of my earlier opinion that a man in your position at the present time is under no obligation to join the colors."

When war comes, Knox continued, "that will be something different. Under existing circumstances, I can see no reason why you should not regard your duties to your wife and to your little children as of primary importance." As for the Chicago Daily News' highly regarded foreign service, Knox told him there were no openings, but he was sure his Chicago editors would keep B.J. in mind.

Of course, the war did come. Already enveloping Europe and the Pacific, it caught up with the United States just months after Knox's April note to B.J.

The war came first not from the expected source: Hitler's Nazi Germany, which had brazenly rearmed itself despite World War I treaties forbidding it to do so. Even as he began his mass roundup and killing of Jews, Hitler was rolling over neighboring nations. With Knox's help, President Roosevelt was assisting the United Kingdom–which stood alone in Europe after the fall of France and Poland. They worked around prevailing American isolationist sentiment and policies. Their Lend-Lease agreement allowed the U.S. to provide Britain with older warships in exchange for 99-year leases to British bases in the Atlantic, including Bermuda. FDR also ordered Knox and the Navy to step up its patrols in the North Atlantic, where German submarines and aircraft were menacing American-British trade.

But the Empire of Japan struck the first surprise blow against America. Its shock Sunday attack on Pearl Harbor decimated the U.S. Pacific Fleet. Numerous hints, signals—and even decoded messages that Japan would not long abide American efforts to contain its efforts to rule in the Pacific—were either missed or ignored. Somehow, too, in the fog of war, FDR, Knox, and others in Washington missed being held to account for the security failures that left Pearl Harbor a sitting duck.

Back in New Hampshire in May 1942, B.J. received a letter from Paul Scott Mowrer, editor of the Chicago Daily News, telling him that "you can try to get to Russia, if you wish…" but Mowrer didn't encourage it. The news service already had a reporter there, so McQuaid would have to stick strictly to the air story.

"Alaska would be worth a trip if you can make the proper arrangements," Mowrer suggested.

Mowrer had been a correspondent during the First Balkan War, as well as World War I. He won the first Pulitzer Prize in the field of foreign correspondence. His brother, Edgar Ansel Mowrer, was also a foreign correspondent. Paul's son, Richard, was, like B.J., part of the CDN foreign service during World War II.[1]

Paul Scott Mowrer was married to Hadley Hemingway, the first wife of Ernest Hemingway. Like many of his colleagues, my father was not a fan of the famous author. The two briefly shared a tent in France in the summer of 1944. Hemingway was also reporting on the war. B.J. told me that he found him a pompous blowhard.

Arrangements for B.J. to get to Alaska included getting his passport updated to include permission to travel throughout the Pacific. He received inoculations and vaccinations per War Department procedure. He also received permission from his local draft board in Chicago to leave the country for a period of six months to visit the Hawaiian Islands and any ports touched by the U.S. Navy's Pacific Fleet. That permission became a semi-annual routine for the duration of the war.

The Navy issued him official accreditation to the Pacific Fleet. War correspondents fell under the military in all respects, particularly in censoring their news stories and access to battlefields. They wore officers' uniforms and were technically classified as the lowest officer rank. When in the field, correspondents were billeted with other junior officers, had access to the officers' mess, and were provided military transport as available.

They weren't permitted firearms, although some would claim to have had and used them. Their uniforms differed depending on whether they were with the Army or Navy. A "war correspondent" armband was required. The rules were spelled out in booklets issued by both the Army and Navy. As with military personnel,

---

1   After retiring, Paul and Hadley Mowrer moved to Choc-orua, New Hampshire. Paul became the state's first poet laureate. The two remained friends with B.J.

the correspondents were subject to censorship of their personal
letters as well, much to Peg McQuaid's chagrin and occasional
outrage as the war progressed.

A few correspondents were staff reporters for just one newspaper,
usually a big metro daily. Others, like McQuaid, worked for
news syndicates. Many newspapers relied on a syndicate such
as Chicago's to augment national or world coverage from the
Associated Press, United Press, or Hearst's International News
Service.

More than 1,600 U.S. correspondents would receive some
form of accreditation from the Allies, but the number who
would report from the front lines was much lower. In his book,
Reporting War, former foreign correspondent Ray Moseley
cites a figure of 69 killed either on the battlefield or through
disease or accidents. "By the end of the war," Moseley notes,
"2.2 percent of American reporters had been killed and 6.8
percent wounded, compared with 2.5 percent and 4.2 percent
for the American military."

In Look magazine in 1945, columnist Marquis Childs wrote of
war correspondents:
   "If there is anything a fighting man has done in this war that
   a war correspondent has failed to do, I do not know what it
   is…The number of war correspondents killed is far greater
   in proportion than the number of deaths among combat
   troops. That is because their own zeal to see it themselves,
   to be there when it happens, drives them into the face of
   danger. …Battle reporters on the job have the hardboiled
   nonchalance of the fighting man. Outwardly they take
   themselves and their work with the utmost casualness. That,
   however, is largely a facade. They are adventure-loving,
   deeply sentimental and insatiably curious. If they weren't,
   of course, they would be writing about something a lot
   quieter and safer than war."

Only a few women were accredited as correspondents, including

B.J.'s CDN colleague Helen Kirkpatrick, but until late in the war, they were forbidden from frontline coverage.

"DON'T FIRE UNTIL YOU SEE THE
SLANTS OF THEIR EYES."

Readers today would cringe at this headline, but not so when it appeared on the front page of the <u>Boston Evening Globe</u> on September 3, 1942. The article was bylined by Bernard J. McQuaid. He had made it to his first front. As editor Mowrer suggested, it was in Alaska, from where U.S. forces were attacking the Aleutian Islands, part of the Alaskan territory, which the Japanese had occupied.

Few Americans had heard of the Aleutians (or Alaska, for that matter). But the islands' proximity to the U.S. West Coast was cause for great concern after the attack on Pearl Harbor. The Japanese were also using the Aleutian campaign to draw U.S. attention away from the enemy's strike on Midway.[2]

For months, McQuaid had this front pretty much to himself. The U.S. Navy's surprise attack on the Aleutian island of Kiska was big news. As McQuaid noted in his story, which was held up for weeks by censors and communications glitches, the attack came on August 6, just eight months after Pearl Harbor.

By October 1942, he told Peg in one letter that he had sent 12 stories to Washington, *"but so far as I know they haven't released any of them yet. I can't see why, myself, since the secret matter contained in them is certainly secret no longer, so far as the Japs are concerned."*

The <u>Globe</u> dedicated almost half its front page to McQuaid's

---

2   The Battle of Midway was a major naval battle in the Pacific Theater of World War II that took place June 4-7, 1942, six months after the Empire of Japan's attack on Pearl Harbor and one month after the Battle of the Coral Sea

account, which the paper preceded with several smaller headline decks and an editor's note hailing the "Boston reporter."

Next to his photo, the note read:

This stirring dispatch was pounded out aboard a United States cruiser by a 32-year-old [he was 34] New Englander who has been trying to be where the news is breaking ever since he was a youngster in Candia, N.H., where his wife and two small children are now living with his mother. Son of Elias McQuaid, for many years chief editorial writer of the <u>Boston American,</u> and brother of Elias McQuaid, now on the <u>American,</u> Bernard was a copy boy every possible vacation day on Manchester and Boston newspapers while studying at St. Anselm's.

Later he went to Georgetown University and the University of Chicago. As a reporter his early interest in aviation sent him on the test flight of the world's first plastic plane in Nashua in 1935. He joined the Boston Globe-Chicago Daily News foreign staff six months ago and was the first newspaperman permitted to look over the Canadian and American patrol and ferry bases in Newfoundland and Labrador. Two of McQuaid's four brothers are in the Navy.

Another McQuaid brother would soon join the Navy, and brother Elias would enlist in the Army. But just two, Bernard and Joe (serving as a Navy supply officer in the Pacific), saw frontline action.

McQuaid's story described the American attack as one in which fog that **"old dirty, disgusting, miserable, obscene fog"** as initially the enemy. **"Do these so-and- Japs make their own weather? 'What the hell is this, some type of a secret weapon?'"** he wrote, paraphrasing unnamed sailors.

But the fog bank suddenly lifted. The U.S. ships could see their target, attack it, and then retreat into the fog that was now **"that delightful fog bank; that good, old friendly praiseworthy**

pro-American fog bank; not made in Tokio [sic] after all."
He wrote of guns from nearby ships firing and then of his own
destroyer's guns **"speaking in tones neither delayed nor
muffled. These were ours. They pounded our ears like some
brass-knuckled Briareus."**

Globe editors inserted a parenthetical note "for the benefit of
Bostonians" to explain that "Briareus was, according to the
dictionary, formerly engaged in throwing thunderbolts with
Zeus."

The Americans suffered no deaths and only a single minor
casualty in the initiative. In its aftermath, McQuaid wrote that
on his ship, **"men relieved from the long watch at battle
stations stuff themselves with coffee and sandwiches.**

"Yet, here and there," he observed, **"a man sits quietly, apart
from the melee of conversation, eyes shut and hands limp on
the chair arms, enjoyinged that perfection of relaxation that
comes after the nervous and physical delights of extreme
tension.**

**"You know exactly what he sees with those closed eyes of
his,"** McQuaid told his readers, **"Because you see the same
things yourself when you close your eyes."**

The Aleutian campaign was little known, then or now, to
most Americans. Even the soldiers and sailors sent there were
kept in the dark as to where they were headed. And they were
assigned there for long periods without rotations that were
normal elsewhere. Living conditions were primitive. Sub-
zero temperatures and incessant fog were dominant features.
Resupply was a constant problem.

In his book The Thousand-Mile War, Brian Garfield listed some
of the effects: "Tired, ill-supplied, ill-fed, they lived on their
nerves. The contrast was striking between the clean-shaven faces
of the new replacements and the hard, lined faces of the young

veterans…. Dr. Benjamin Davis recalls, 'There was a terrific shortage of proper food. We never had any but powdered milk and eggs in the twenty-nine months I was up there. Bad food ruined the men's teeth…When I finally got back to Anchorage I had my mouth X-rayed and found that every tooth in my mouth was abscessed. I left all my teeth in Alaska.'"

A running joke had it that the quick way to defeat the Japanese was to feed them the same food that American servicemen were served. Fortunately, B.J. was a bit better off, returning to mainland Alaska on occasion. His war trunk contains two receipts for steaks (medium) purchased and consumed at the Naval Air Station in Kodiak.

THE HOME FRONT

Aug. 24, 1942

My darling,
Can you imagine me writing a letter at quarter of
seven in the morning? I'm at the Candia Improvement
club all by my lonesome, been here since six o'clock
and am on duty until twelve this noon. The entire state
is going to have a black-out some time this week, so
they asked for volunteers in town here. [The blackout
occurred two days later.] Polly Wyman called me, and
I offered to take this morning's shift. The women are
doing the day shifts and the men at night.

Whether the Japanese or the Germans had plans to destroy Candia, New Hampshire, as part of their prosecution of the war seems doubtful to me, but my mother wrote that the work made her feel useful.

I've done nothing so far since the war started so
thought I could at least give six hours of my time
to help out here. I relieved Eliot Wyman, and also
delivered your message to him…

*We are all looking forward to reading your articles in
the paper. I'm busting to know when and where you
have been. I still get a sick feeling at the bottom of my
stomach when I think of you being under fire.*

*Oh darling, I'm so very proud of you, and worried
about you all in the same breath.*

She told him what she was seeing on the home front.
*Some [people] realize only too well that there is a war
going on but of course there are others that need a
bombing or two to wake them up to the fact and I'm
not so sure that the time isn't too far away for that to
happen either.*

*What the hell can we do about it darling—I'd like
nothing better than to stand on a soap box and rant on
for hours.*

She wondered what was happening with all the war material
supposedly being produced.
*Half the camps in the country don't even have enough
rifles to go around so that the boys can even practice
target shooting.*

B.J. had written that he did not know what was happening
elsewhere in the world, but Peg told him that neither did the
folks back home:

*We read sugarcoated versions of what is happening
mostly from London – but Stoneman [a fellow CDN
correspondent] had an article last week telling what a
mess of hokum the London papers are parsing out to
the British. Everything is a hell of a mess, but you are
wrong darling if you think we are all having a good
time and taking it easy – at least not in New England,
most of us aren't.*

*People around here are nervous, depressed, and half
scared to death. They are going to ration meat next—
nobody seems to know about the fuel oil situation and
a few people are sensible enough to expect an air raid
anytime now. Most of us live from one day to the next
and try not to think too much about the future. Darling
if it weren't for the fact that I have our two children to
look after I'd be out myself getting a Jap's ear or so –
and it wouldn't be pickled either.*

The <u>Boston Globe</u> incorrectly noted in B.J.'s Kiska story that
Peg was living with her mother-in-law. She wasn't. She stayed
in their South Road home, dismissing B.J.'s suggestion that she
might move in with his folks if it turned very cold.

His widowed mother, Arethusa Bean McQuaid, also wrote a
letter that August to her *Dear Bernie Boy*. She filled him in on
his sister and four brothers and his own young family.

"Peg is fine and the children. Judy had fallen jumping off a
stump," she told him, but her cast was now off, and she was
well. "She says, 'Daddy is bringing me some big thing when he
comes home, bigger than this house. Guess it will be a pony.'

"Johnny is running around everywhere now. When he comes
down he'll start for the pantry and begin hollering 'cookie
cookie' and 'drink of water.'"

She told B.J. that Peg seemed "weary at times with you gone
and her Dad and all. But we go back and forth and [she] keeps
up her courage."

Peg's father, John F. Griffin, just 62, died suddenly from a heart
attack on April 18, 1942, shortly before B.J. moved his family
back to Candia.

Arethusa still had two of her four cows, she wrote, and guessed
she could manage them pretty well.

Cynthia Dolan, one of B.J.'s first cousins, "is working in a Baltimore Md. Defense factory," his mother wrote. She was among the many young, unmarried women eager to help the war effort. Also, like a lot of them, she would meet and marry a handsome young officer, Paul Hughes, who would go off to the war and die in combat in the European theater.

It wouldn't be until the first Kiska story saw print that his family had any idea where B.J. was. Peg wrote that she saw his piece in the Manchester and Boston newspapers and that friends had told her how good a story it was. She also showed another of his stories to family, neighbors, and friends. This one, in the monthly Coronet magazine, was written months earlier, before B.J. had gone to the front. The story was about American and Canadian air force efforts to defend against possible enemy attacks from Germany or Japan. He had been paid well for the effort and sent the money on to Peg.

Others in the family noticed the articles as well.

"You have been getting famous as all hell, as Peg has probably informed you," wrote his brother, Dave, now stationed with the Navy in Portland, Maine. Dave tweaked his older brother about being called a Boston reporter: "When Boston, the Hub of the universe and seat of culture, starts claiming anybody for its very own, you have arrived–at least several days previously."

Candia was mentioned, Dave noted, as well as their father and Elias, Jr. "But the last line made Joe and I feel very insignificant, indeed, referring to himself and their younger brother.

"Now I'll have to go out and strangle a U-boat singlehanded," Dave joked. Turning serious, he cautioned his brother to be careful: "I gather, from reading your stuff, that you are seeing how a naval war is fought from the inside out, and that you have had your share of close shaves. I certainly wouldn't risk my neck any more than I had to, if I were you.

"It appears to me, from reading some war correspondents' stuff, that they keep themselves at a fairly safe distance from actual hostilities and interview the boys when they get back from the front or a task force assignment. That doesn't make for such colorful writing, I know, but it must save considerable wear and tear on the person, to put it mildly."

Dave noted that *the Colonel* [Knox] had recently paid tribute to newsmen for the risks they were taking: "He was motivated by publication of a list of casualties among newspapermen, about 30 of whom have been killed, wounded or captured. He said he had had difficulty in 'restraining' some of his own men who wanted to go along on every kind of assignment, even the most dangerous."

Dave reported that another McQuaid brother, Arthur, Joe's twin, had been sworn into the Navy but not placed yet. When Arthur was placed, it would be disastrous for him and the McQuaid family. Dave had worked for the Manchester newspaper as a state house reporter before he entered the service. He told B.J. that "the draft is cleaning out a lot of the Union-Leader's personnel. "

Over the next few months, McQuaid's Aleutian stories would begin a pattern he followed throughout the war, providing both big-picture and small-detail perspectives.

ABOARD A U.S. WARSHIP
IN ALEUTIAN WATERS, September [1942]:

Summer is dying in the Bering Sea. Over Kiska way, Autumn leaves are falling on the Japs. But that's a story in itself. You see, there are no trees on Kiska.

These leaves were a variety of the old British trick of dropping 'leaflets' dressed up to fit Jap psychology. Seems the Japs have a frightful superstition about leaves falling from heaven. So somebody has rigged up a lot of imitation

leaves, and the planes fly over Kiska and heave out bundles of them. They have Jap characters written on them but no one up this way seems to know just what the characters mean. Everybody is mildly anxious to see if the trick works, and the Japs start showing any evil effects. Meantime, fortunately, we have not abandoned the less romantic custom of dropping bombs.

In a follow-up piece, he told readers, "**As you might expect, somebody in Washington cooked up the idea, and prepared the imitation leaves, which were forwarded here for delivery by the pilots.**"

The inscription on the fake leaves included a promise that American bombs would soon rain down on Kiska in far greater quantity than the Kiri leaves.

At the time, we were establishing our big new airbase 200 miles away. Soon, sure enough the bombs did start falling, just as advertised. The Japs are still on Kiska, despite bombs and Kiri leaves, but there's a universal feeling that they can't hang on there long, unless they deliberately decide to sacrifice 20 to 50 percent of the shipping they send in to supply the place.

Maybe that leaf stunt was a kind of cute trick, at that.

B.J. also wrote about games that sailors devised to pass the time. They called one Hernia ball.

It was nothing but an overgrown medicine ball, but when wet, as it usually is, it is a formidable instrument weighing in at around 25 pounds. It acquires its odd title by virtue of the game we play with it, which is a cross between volley ball and mass mayhem.

Hernia Ball is this ship's most popular 'recreatin.' Nearly

all the officers play it, and the men have organized a league. (A team of marines, as you might expect, are league leaders at present.)

To play Hernia Ball, we stretch a tennis net between our Number Three gun turret and the lower bridge superstructure. Netted backstops keep the ball, and occasionally the players, from going over the side.

Some people get on one side of the net and some on the other. One takes the ball and hurls it downward across the six-foot high net with such violence, or guile, that it strikes the deck before the opposing side can catch it. If they do catch it, they try to do the same thing.

There are practically no rules to this interesting game. Considerable bodily contact develops at the net, whither both sides rush ferociously in an effort to score, or to wrest the ball from an opponent. Pushing, shoving, blocking, clipping, straight-arming, tripping, holding and ball-stealing are quite good form. Biting and eye-gouging find almost no support.

Certain supermanishly robust individuals who seem to find their way into our navy in considerable numbers are capable of taking this 25-pound missile, the hernia ball, in one hand, and firing it across the net like a pitched baseball, putting a little spin on it for good measure. No one who has stopped one of these shots with his chin retains the slightest respect for a Jap 14-inch gun or heavy bomb. We seem, moreover, to prefer to play this game in 55-knot gales accompanied by driving rains, while the ships roll at angles of 20 degrees and upward.

We are undoubtedly crazy, but when something occurs to interfere with our daily Hernia ball game at its appointed hour we all feel bitter; something like we do when we run out of movie films (and the re-fueling tanker turns up without any replacements [taken out by censor]). **Yesterday there was an air alert. These are common enough out here, but this one looked like the real McCoy. The planes were seen clearly on the horizon, coming for us hellbent, and no one could identify them. On all sides, shipmates began cursing and defaming the Japanese, not for attacking us, but for busting up the ballgame.**

It turned out that the planes were B-24s and P-38s on the way out to drop some autumn leaves on the Japs at Kiska. It made us all feel so good to see our own fighters for the first time in this Aleutian war that we didn't mind the postponement of the Hernia ball game.

The following sentence, crossed out by the censors, read:
These ships have been carrying on this campaign without any air protection now for about four months, which must be some kind of a record in this war.

In another piece, B.J. began with a soft focus aboard an ancient destroyer that had been converted to status as an aviation tender, **"nursing the huge patrol planes that fly daily search and reconnaissance missions through North Pacific combat zones.**

"She is a floating home for their pilots and crews, a handy garage and filling station for the planes themselves. She is a communications center – a liaison point for land, sea and air operations, and between Army and Navy."

He extolled the ship's comforts, including the hot showers that offered great relief to Army pilots billeted in tents on land: **They come out from the beach in small boats, carrying their towels and shaving kits with them, and she takes them on in daily relays as long as her water holds out.**

In late-night musings to me years later, my father would share his opinion that the Navy had it all over the Army for creature

comforts in wartime. You might get sunk, he said, but you always had three meals a day, hot showers, and clean laundry.
In the destroyer piece, his calm opening narrative turned suddenly harrowing. Abruptly awakened and tumbled half out of his bunk by what he thought was a torpedo, he went topside. He told readers that a **"sudden 60-knot gale had knocked the ship from its mooring buoy.**

"The ship always had its engines running, so this would not have been a terrible problem. But the cove in which the ship was moored was jammed with shipping, including a couple of transports unloading cargo, and several patrol planes.

As our searchlight picks up the planes, we see that they are less than 300 feet away, and we are riding right down on them.

"Someone recalls aloud that some of the enlisted crewmen are living aboard the planes. Doubtless these youngsters are snoring in their bunks, unaware of the terrible danger that hovers near them."

He wrote that the ship's skipper had determined the only course of action that could avert tragedy. **"Our engines are backing full speed astern."**

Then B.J. teased readers, asking, **"Will the propellors take hold in time to save the PBYs?**

"The suspense endures briefly, but the decisive 30 seconds seems eternity itself. There are 50 feet to spare when the props grip and our sidewise motion halts. Slowly, with a throb and a quiver as of some live thing in pain, the ship begins backing off."

With one crisis averted, another loomed in the form of two ships just aft of (behind) the destroyer, which now must thread its way between them:

We make it with eight feet of leeway between the schooner's bow and our starboard beam. Comfortably clear, we put our engines ahead and ride easily again, bow into the wind.

OF LETTERS AND LONGINGS

Tuesday night, Jan. 12, 1943

Bernie darling – This ceases to be funny – aren't you getting my letters at all? Received your cable last Sunday when I got home from church, and I answered it immediately by Western Union – did you get that? Well, I'll keep on with my weekly epistles

about the doings of the McQuaids on South Rd – somebody must be reading them anyway.

First – there has been a ban placed on pleasure driving in New England – no more of it for anyone. We can only use our cars for church and business. That really is a laugh on three gallons of gas per week, especially out here in the country. However it doesn't affect me in the least – my weekly trip to the city on Friday and church on Sundays and a sneak trip over to your mother's every other week or so is all I've been able to do for some time anyway. We did manage to get to the movies three times this fall, but that is something of the past now. This ban is going to ruin the skiing I guess – most of the places up north have closed for the duration.

Johnny and I went in town last Friday morning and had a session at the barber shop. I simply had to have his hair cut or buy him a violin. He yelled and screamed according to form, and I had to sit in the chair and hold him, getting a mouthful of hair in the bargain. I had the barber cut it short and he looks like a regular boy now – adorably – wish you could

*see him. We went up to Galways after lunch and Aunt
Katherine took care of the baby while I had my hair
done and brought my week's supply of food.*

*Sunday afternoon Judy and I took our skates and
walked down to Wyman's. Polly and Eliot and I cleared
off some ice in the field next to their house – and with
Lois and Judy, we skated for more than an hour. They
asked us to stay for dinner, which we did, then Judy
and I walked home. I've been lame as an old horse
yesterday and today – but the exercise did me good –
only hope I can get more of it this weekend.*

*There is a new school teacher in town – third and
fourth grade, and she is living up at Doc. Davis'. Mrs.
Davis called me last week and asked if I would rent the
other half of the barn to her (teacher) so that she could
keep her car under cover. I told her I'd be glad to let
her keep it there free of charge – so she is using it now
– I don't need it and I thought it would be pretty small
to make her pay rent – don't you dear?*

*Well sweetheart nothing more for tonight. Judy and
Johnny are both fine and Judy still goes to school every
day. Johnny keeps me busy all day – trying to keep an
eye on him. We all love you and miss you, but we can
carry on as long as you can.*

*Do hope my letters will reach you sometime in the near
future – seems useless scribbling away, knowing that
you haven't read one of them yet. If you do happen to
get one I wish you would check up and see what the
trouble is, will you darling? Please write soon again –
I love you, Peg.*

[From B.J.'s Nov. 6, 1943, letter to Peg in which he wasn't
certain if he would make it home for Christmas, but wanted to
make sure he was home for a special anniversary in February.]

*Did the service ever carry that story I wrote last
February 22nd, on which date I was flying a strike
mission (which never found anything to strike) from the
Enterprise, in a torpedo plane, in a magic South Seas
dawn? And all I could think about was a snowbank in
the New Hampshire mountains? I wrote it, especially
for you, and expected you to comment on it, but you
never did.*

In fact, the CDN did carry B.J.'s story. The <u>Manchester Union</u>
ran it, so Peg likely saw it.

**The cloudbanks took on fanciful shapes. There was a
rugged, bewigged profile of George Washington. In lifelike
majesty, the cloud portrait of Washington stared out
over the Pacific that is being conquered by his sons. This
reminded me that it was Washington's birthday, which is
by way of being an anniversary of some special significance
in this correspondent's family. Several years ago to the
day, Mrs. McQuaid and I were skiing in the Pawtuckaway
mountains…Perhaps Peg and the children are skiing there
today.**

**A matter of small public interest no doubt but it has its
point as a typical case of what is known as "doping off" in
an airplane. Pilots have been known to do this, as well as
hitchhiking reporters. The formation wheeled sharply and
dove and I came back from the New Hampshire snowbanks
to the realities of war in the sultry Southwest.**

IN THE SOUTH PACIFIC, FEB. 24 [1943]–

**From 17,000 feet we hurtled down out of the sun at 500 feet
per second. It was a vertical dive. We held it all the way
down to the bomb-release point at about 2,000 feet. The
pull-out was not at all the painful sensation one had been
led to expect. There was no blackout, not even a dimout.**

The pilot distributed the leveling off process over 1,000 feet of altitude. The "G-load" couldn't have been more than four or five. Physiologically, this was about as much strain as a ride on a roller coaster.

Psychologically, that 30-second plummet drop from the deep sky to the sea was a little nerve-wracking. In fact, you became pretty well convinced, just before the pullout, that the pilot had forgotten about that little detail.

You wondered whether you ought to remind him of it through the intercom phone, but noticing how the altimeter needle spun around, you doubted there would be time to do so because the ocean looked terribly big and close and brittle.

But after the second or third dive – from lesser altitudes, 6,000 to 9,000 feet – you got used to it and began to enjoy it. After that first breathtaking dive from the oxygen levels, it was impossible not to have confidence in the ability of the rugged little Douglas dive bomber to "take it." As for your pilot – a 22-year-old ensign from Raleigh, N.C. – you were able to forget his youth and the fact that he got out of flight school less than a year ago. You remembered instead that he was a successful veteran of combat engagements in which he had scored hits on enemy warships, and eluded flocks of pursuing Zeros.

All these pilots and radio-gunners of the bomber squadron are veterans of one or more engagements. Playing cribbage and chess in the carrier wardroom, most of them seem shockingly young and immature. Up there in the hot tropical sky, whipping those 12 Douglass's through the precision evolution of tight formations; "peeling off" for their long dives; joining up again in formation as they twist and dodge low over the sea, you accept them for what they are – undisputed masters of one of the most difficult and hazardous professions; the best diver bombs in the world.

And you land back on the carrier with a tremendous respect for the simple professional integrity and competence which is required in a 22-year-old boy who goes out to fight this kind of war.

CHAPTER TWO

READERS, RATIONING

Peg and the kids at home in Candia.

FOR MANY READERS, B.J. McQuaid's most important stories were not about the big picture of the war but about those fighting it; and not so much about Army generals or Navy captains, although he wrote about many of those. The stories that mattered most to many were the ones that mentioned and often quoted their loved ones: individual GIs, aviators, Marines, submariners, Navy seamen, and Seabees.

These stories mattered to families, friends, and even former teachers back home.

"So many reports are general and the individuals of each organization are not mentioned." wrote a mother from Macon, Georgia, whose son was on an LCT[3] during the Normandy

---

3 A landing craft for tanks.

landings. McQuaid had done a piece on the craft, nicknamed the "No Gum Chum."

It was a fine description and should be recorded for history, she told him: "War correspondents are surely doing a job and certainly are exposing themselves to great danger in order to bring the news in[to] American homes while it is news."

Dec. 10, '42

My dear Mr. McQuaid,
I see by the Daily News that you are back in Chicago so I am passing along to you 'bits' of appreciation for the article appearing in the Nov. 13 issue in which you spoke of the 'very human'...Major Don Dunlap.

It was indeed a most pleasant surprise to come across the name of Don Dunlap who had been a very splendid student in my classes in geography in a Teachers College in western Pennsylvania. I knew that he took up flying following his graduation but had not heard of him for some time so it was a real pleasure to have word of him.

I believe it was during his last year in college that his twin brother was killed in air maneuvers. Some, I recall, tried to dissuade him from flying."

The writer, Edna Gray, told McQuaid that she sent his story to Dunlap's wife as well as to his mother, and both had replied. The mother told Gray how much the story meant to her: "Our news through his letters has been so meager, that it was refreshing to get that chatty bit from a news reporter."

The mother also told Gray that "she is very sure he will do his best and his best will be good." Gray added her own words of praise. "I think you reporters are doing a splendid job and by including names of men with interesting bits of news about them

are giving more cheer to those at home than you may realize."
Another mom, Mrs. Fred Croft of Illinois, told McQuaid how
interested she was in his articles on the work of LSTs in the
Southwest Pacific.[4] She sent several stories to her son, an
executive officer and then skipper of LST 339. She quoted her
son's response.

"The articles by M'Quaid are exceedingly interesting and
have been avidly read by us all," he wrote. He told her that the
censors or the Navy Department wouldn't let the crew write
such details as McQuaid had reported but "it is a fact that the
author was a pretty conscientious reporter–except of course in
his prejudice or preference for ships. Naturally, he thinks most
of his own ship."

Mrs. Croft thanked McQuaid for his reports. "When they pass
muster with the boys themselves, they must be good."

B.J. didn't hide his own admiration for the young men he
covered. He described the aftermath of a bruising storm at sea
in the Aleutians for one ship's crew:
**We have averted disaster after a gale that snapped us from
our mooring. From the forecastle deck, men of the special
set detail turn a questioning gaze up to the bridge. Their
young, patient, gale-stung faces, glistening in the blue glare
of the searchlight, outshine the slick surfaces of their own
oilskins.**

**A vast surge of affection and admiration for these 18-and
20-year-olds–boys in years, but tough, reliable seamen in
determination and experience, wells up. What a beating
they are taking, out on that narrow, completely exposed
deck, where it is job enough, in the teeth of this hurricane,**

----

4. The bigger brother of LCTs, these were Landing Ships for

Tanks.

just to keep from being blown over the side. But they are far from being sorry for themselves. Officers and men alike are evidently exhilarated by this chips-down battle with the worst the northern sea has to offer.

Others noticed B.J.'s work as well. One was a U.S. Marine Corps combat correspondent, Tech. Sgt. Maurice E. Moran of Pittsburgh, Pennsylvania. He sent the following item to the Chicago Daily News in October 1943:

Guadalcanal–(Delayed)–Barney McQuaide [sic] is the forty-oddish sort of a citizen you'd expect to find behind a bank teller's window. Or at his club clucking dismally and chortling happily, according to the trend of war news he was scanning.

But his natural habitat these days is a rain-drenched fox-hole in some God-forsaken jungle. He's one of that gallant band of reporters who make war headlines and risk their necks to do it.

Barney represents Chicago Daily News Service. He and such guys as Richard Tregaskis, International News, J. Norman Lodge and Lief [Leif] Erickson of the Associated Press and Byron Taves, of the United Press fight the war with typewriters, for which the American public can be everlastingly grateful.

A tiny by-line at the top of a graphic description of blood, suffering and heroism is their only material reward, other than a salary which means nothing to most of them.

When Jap bombs blast the breath of death–they're there, in a fox-hole perhaps with lizards and spiders as company.

When each step into a dense jungle might mean the ominous rattle of a machine gun ambush–they're there."

B.J. included that item in a letter to Peg:

> *You will notice I appeared 'forty-oddish.' So don't*
> *expect too much when you see me. You will also*
> *noticed [notice] that this Marine apparently thinks*
> *it's a hell of a good thing I'm fighting this war with a*
> *typewriter instead of a gun. Maybe he's got something*
> *there.*

B.J. was 35 when he covered the South Pacific fighting that year.

"LUCKY"

B.J. also kept two letters that were neither to him nor from him. They referenced his stories about a Navy aviator in the Aleutian campaign. At that early point in the war, censorship didn't allow him to identify the flyer by name, but B.J. did note he was from North Dakota.

Fellow aviators in Alaska knew who he was: Lt. William Larson, known as Lucky to his comrades. To fly reconnaissance missions against the Japanese along the island chain, Larson's scout airplane was catapulted from the deck of the USS *Nashville*, a vintage cruiser commanded by U.S. Navy Captain Francis Craven.

A Military Hall of Honor online page explains Lucky this way: William was nicknamed 'Lucky' by the aviator crew of the USS *Nashville*. 'Lucky' participated in several missions off the back of the cruiser. These missions were chronicled by a roving newspaper reporter, B.J. McQuaid, of the Chicago Daily News. One included the story of Lucky's 3,500-foot descent and ocean landing on the Bering Sea under 'pea soup' fog conditions at night. The other tale included Lucky's return after two nights alone in his seaplane, riding out a brutal Alaska storm in a bay while his radioman was stranded on the beach. Lucky saved the naval float plane from damage and the lives of his crew. Both of these stories start out the same, Lucky got lost in the impenetrable fog of the Aleutian Islands, but they illustrate his endurance and aviation judgment that he had honed since growing up on the windswept prairies of North Dakota.

Larson grew up with his brother and parents on a farm in Hanks, North Dakota. McQuaid kept a March 1944 letter that Larson's father, Olaf, wrote to a shipmate of his son. It read: "We have been very grieved and worried over the message we got from the Navy Dept. at Washington on Jan. 4 [1944] saying William is missing in the performance of his duty, and in the service of his country. For some time we did not know what to do. We felt so helpless and dazed. We did not know where William was for sure. But he did tell us about crossing the equator, so we guessed the Solomon Islands, but yet we are not certain."

Olaf told his son's friend that the family had also received a letter from Larson's commanding officer, saying that their son's squadron had been on a bombing tour and that he was soon to get his own squadron. But returning to the combat area from a brief respite, the transport plane on which he was a passenger had crashed. Radio contact with that plane was lost soon after a stop at New Caledonia, and wreckage had been found but no survivors or bodies.

"We are in hopes that he may have reached an island somehow," his father wrote, "and be safe with the natives. Have heard the natives there are friendly towards the U.S. We do not want to believe he is dead. It seems too terrible to think he should have been thru so much–and been pilot himself for over four years, and then go down flying with someone else."

Lucky's brother, Lloyd, was also in the service, Olaf wrote. "So we are alone here on the large farm, and have much stock to care for. Have 800 acres now, thinking the boys would come back and farm. We sure hope this war soon ends, so all the boys can come back safely to their families."

Olaf Larson received a second letter, from Capt. Craven, telling of his son's exploits and saying that he would be asking McQuaid to send the family copies of his two stories. Craven had heard Larson was missing. He wanted the father to know how his son had acquired his nickname, as well as something of his exploits. But there was something more, Craven wrote: "It wasn't luck but great skill, great courage and endurance and splendid judgment which brought your son through those experiences. He was a great aviator, a fine man and a shipmate whom none who served with him in the *Nashville* will forget...I loved him like a son, and I share your distress and grief at what has happened. You can at least be proud to have had such a son."

Lucky's body was never found.

In 2016, B.J.'s two stories about Lucky found their way into Lucky's Life. a book written by Larson's nephew, Don J. Larson. The author told me that while the family wasn't aware of B.J.'s stories when they were published, he was certain that they helped comfort the family when they learned of Lucky's death.

PLUCK AND SKILL RESCUE 'LUCKY' FROM FOGGY SEA
By B.J. M'QUAID

Kodiak, Alaska, July 24–The pilot was known to his shipmates as 'Lucky,' which may have had something to do with it. Nevertheless, the operation was at least 90 percent scientific. For that reason, it should, and no doubt will, go into the record books as an object lesson in lost plane procedure in the open sea.

Lucky got lost through no fault of his, or ours. He'd been up on a routine search flight, from which he'd returned, swift and sure, to his appointed rendezvous with our warship. But when he got there, we were swallowed up in a great bank of

fog–the kind of thing that makes the sea and air operations in these northern waters a business of endless hazard and treachery.

We got him back aboard after he'd been lost nearly three hours. We did it at night, under the same zero-zero conditions that led to his getting lost in the first place.

To appreciate this achievement, it is necessary to understand that the Pacific is a large ocean and that a scout seaplane is a small object. When we finally broke radio silence and discovered Lucky–'sprung him' in the seagoing airman's idiom–he was a good 20 miles astern. Darkness was gathering and the fog, which had been alternately lifting and lowering had settled down for the night. 'Pea soup' gives you no idea.

From the bridge, we could barely make out our forward gun turrets. The problem was to bring the plane in on course, guide it down through 3,000 feet of solid overcast and set it on the sea at a point close enough to the ship to make searching for it something more than a gesture.

All we had was our radio communication with the plane and certain other apparatus, not primarily intended for such use, which enabled us to give Lucky a fairly good notion of the ship's position relative to his own. As for coming down through the soup and landing in the darkness on moderately rough water under zero-zero conditions – that was Lucky's personal problem. We could not help him there.

But we got him over the ship. (We heard his motor, faintly.) And we sent him on down, an estimated five miles or so ahead. We told him to ride it out, for a bit, and we'd be along to pick him up. Our needle was not out of the haystack. All we had left to do was to thread it. Somewhere out ahead, imprisoned by the alabaster wall of fog, Lucky and his radio man sat bobbing on the restless sea. We knew about what their position must have been a few seconds before the landing impact. We knew Lucky would head into the wind and rev his motor enough to hold against the drift, though this would be largely guesswork on his part.

The rub was that if he got as much as a couple hundred feet off our course, we might go on past without ever seeing him.

We came up on the end of our planned run. Still no sign of the plane. One's heart sank. What optimistic fools we were. How could we have expected in all this green-gray vastness of impenetrability, to steer to within a few score feet of the infinitesimally insignificant airplane. At this point one of Lucky's fellow pilots had an idea. A fairly obvious idea, you'll say. Indeed it seemed so to us—as soon as we heard it mentioned. It was the kind of thing that should have been thought of at once, should have been down in the black and white in all elementary procedure manuals.

'Why not have Lucky fire a few bursts from his machine gun?' We waited anxiously for the instruction to go out: GOZ to Lucky; this is GOZ to Lucky. 'Fire a few machine-gun bursts at 30-second intervals. I will repeat. Fire machine gun at intervals 30 seconds. Go ahead.'

Some of us went aft on the bridge and stood in the glare of the lights, our ears straining. The sound came from off our port bow; faintly at first and strong by alteration as the wind fell and quickened. And that was the show.

Within a few seconds a destroyer to port of us had picked up the plane with her light. Soon we saw the little red and green lamps of its wingtips riding up astern. The floats bounced and slid jauntily and defiantly through the following seas. As a final burst of power brought the plane within hoisting range we could see the flames from its exhaust stacks roaring a challenge to the North Pacific and to all fogbanks since the voyage of Noah.

Not all B.J.'s reader mail was positive. He kept a short, handwritten note addressed to him at the <u>Toledo Blade</u>, another newspaper subscriber to CDN reports. It was dated June 7, 1944:

Sir:

Several women called my attention to your article anent politics and paratroopers. They don't believe it and I don't either.

In the first place what would happen to them if they were to come out openly and tell you they were against Roosevelt? If you want the low-down on their real opinions ask their relatives. On second thought, they probably wouldn't tell you either, fearing to harm the boys.

Did you explain the three-point release on parachutes to them as exposed by Drew Pearson?[5]

I'll bet your name isn't M'Quaid either. Why are the American people treated as morons and fed so much rubbish when newsprint is scarce? More persons have expressed themselves as nauseated at the 'tripe' fed us.

Sincerely, Eva S. Tomb
1704 Circular Rd.
Toledo, Ohio.

The story of which Mrs. Tomb was critical was written in England just days before D-Day. B.J. had received permission to talk politics with a paratroop group [that] was "**handpicked**

---

5. Syndicated <u>Washington Post</u> columnist Pearson had written of a stateside incident that spring in which eight paratroopers drowned, at least in part, he reported, because of their complex parachute release. The British had a much simpler one-step release.

for my benefit to represent all geographical sections of America and practically all racial and national origins."

Most of them distinguished between the Nazis and Germans in general, although they all said Germany would need **"long-term police occupation to prevent it from ever again building an army, navy or air force."** They had a simple solution for the Japanese problem: it was to obliterate all Japanese.

What apparently upset Mrs. Tombs was this line:
While they thought {Republican Tom] Dewey a 'smart politician' and admired his vote-getting capabilities, they were without exception against changing horses in midstream and thought Roosevelt ought to be reelected in appreciation of the fine job he has done in this war.

COPING ON THE HOME FRONT

When 900 women crowd in to try to buy 240 pairs of nylon hose, something is bound to bust. At the James W. Hill company, this morning, something did.

It was three glass show cases in front of the stocking counter, which found the pressure just too much. Fortunately, none of the women in the front row were cut, store officials said.

Despite the crash, however, not one woman moved out of line and those in back kept trying to get within reaching distance of the count.

"'Honest,' Med Chandler, store manager said, 'I was almost afraid to let the crowd in this morning when I saw the women lined up across the sidewalk before 9 o'clock. Women were required to turn in a pair of silk or nylon hose for each one purchased. Sales of nylon were limited to one per customer.'"
–The <u>Manchester Leader</u>, November 11, 1942.

Early in the war, rationing became a fact of life for most Americans, including Peg and her kids. At one point, much to her aggravation, a lack of oil forced the local school to shut down for two weeks.

> *The school,* she wrote to B.J., *has put in their order for grates so as to connect to coal, but nobody seems to know when they will get them or anything about it. "* It meant the school year would last longer.

Peg continued:

> *Serves the school board right–they were warned last fall to connect if they could but they decided to risk it and now see what has happened–the kids will have to pay for it, not those old stuffed shirts!*

Their daughter wasn't bothered, though. Judy got to spend time with B.J.'s mother.

> *Ma is lonesome with everyone gone, and I think she really enjoys having Judy around the place with her.*

Peg told B.J. that school officials had not planned correctly. But she had:

> *Today I sent in my application for oil for the year. We had to fill out a lot of papers and also measure the length and width of every room in the house that is to be heated–what a job. Can't buy any more oil until we get our ration books and then we don't know how much we will be allowed. [A teenage brother of one of her friends in Candia helped her with the measuring].*

> Coffee would be rationed soon too, *I'll be darned glad of it and only wish they had started it earlier. I have exactly one half a pound now and can't buy anymore at any of the stores in town.*

She noted that a neighbor had 15 pounds of coffee stored away:
> *They are the worst hoarders yet. I'm really quite*
> *surprised at their attitude...*

When B.J. inquired in a further letter about rationing, Peg told him:
> *Please don't worry about us here at home–things aren't*
> *really tough at least not for the McQuaids on South*
> *Road. I still get three gallons of gas a week–haven't*
> *run out of oil yet, and so far have managed to buy one*
> *pound of butter a week and sometimes two, also meat,*
> *which is a lot more than other people get. You should*
> *see the lines in front of Kennedys butter story [in*
> *Manchester] every day when they have butter–two and*
> *three blocks long and if they are lucky they get one-*
> *quarter lb. and no more... the secret of my success is*
> *this–no more buying at chain stores or the Star Market.*
> *No butter for me–no business from me.*

Instead, like another neighbor, she switched to a smaller store which kept her better supplied. She also spent two or three dollars a week at a Candia store, *just enough to keep on the good side so that when he gets butter in, he saves me a pound.*

> *We are just about the only ones in Candia and most*
> *of Manchester who are not eating margarine at the*
> *present time. But they say that they are going to ration*
> *butter in the spring. If the darned fools had only done*
> *it a long time ago there wouldn't have been this acute*
> *shortage.*

Two years later, in Normandy, B.J. would write that some newly liberated French civilians seemed to have "**most personal bitterness against the German rationing system and particularly their inability to get ration tickets for butter.**

"**They sounded,**" he observed, "**almost like good American housewives at this point.**"

Even before rationing began for Peg, many items were in short supply. Tea was scarce, bananas were a luxury item, and eggs cost sixty cents a dozen.

> *We all just grit out teeth and keep on, thanking our lucky stars that we still have money enough to buy food and fuel. Nobody does much kicking, and shouldn't– there isn't a family left that doesn't have some member out in one of the four corners of the earth and as long as we win this damn war we can survive all right–we here at home can take it too–don't forget that.*

Margaret Callahan, Peg's aunt, and the head of accounting at the Union and Leader newspapers, also wrote to B.J.:

"Peg is doing a swell job, Bernie, not alone looking after her children but planning the running of her home and adjusting herself to business conditions which is certainly a new field for her. Ration[ing] of oil, food and gasoline creates many problems, but everyone has taken it in stride and managing to get along very nicely. She had to tote around more than once on the oil situation, but always managed to come out on top...It was a cruel, hard winter with the thermometer dropping to levels that broke sixty-three and seventy-three-year records.

Those record-low temperatures and repeated snowstorms could make things lonely for a young mother. A January 1943 sleet storm knocked out the electricity. Peg told B.J. that she and her live-in helper, a teenaged girl, *"were both fit to be tied"* as they had just *"settled down to listen to Duffy's Tavern on the radio."*

> *We've had a hard winter–several bad storms and below zero weather again last week. (She) bought another cord of wood from Otto Pearson the other day–that old kitchen range is still a god-send believe me.*

One month later, in February 1943, while B.J. was reporting of flying off an aircraft carrier in the South Pacific, Peg's letter to him continued the storm news.

> *Monday morning the wind was howling and the temperature had dropped to fifteen below zero, so they called off school and Judy was home all day. This morning the temperature was thirty-two below on South Rd. and forty below in the village so they called off school again all over the state... Your mother called me this morning and said they were freezing over there–that house is never warm, and am I glad I'm in my own house darling–I'd die if I had to stay there all the time.*

Life on the home front also included death. Peg was coping with overseeing her father's estate and the sale of his Manchester home. The deaths of Candia residents also figured into her weekly letters.

> *Oct. 7, 1942.*

> *Mr. Bickford died last Saturday, and Mrs. Charter, Gene's wife, died suddenly Tuesday afternoon of a heart attack. I helped Paulina and Lillian Seward lift Mrs. Charter from the rocking chair, in which they found her dead, on to a couch.*
> *Paulina stopped here on her way up after they had called her on the phone and asked me to go with her. She was scared to pieces but it didn't bother me any–I guess I'm hardened to that business after all these years.*

Peg kept B.J. posted on his family as well. His sister, Eileen, *has been in bed for three weeks–vomiting her head off every time she tries to eat.*

> *She swears she has intestinal flu, I swear she is*

pregnant, and your mother and Bob [Harris, Eileen's
husband] just swear.

Peg was right, although her sister-in-law would miscarry.

Ever since childhood, Arthur McQuaid had seemed a bit odd.
Peg didn't think entering the military would change that, and
she was right about that, too. Like brothers Dave and Joe, Arthur
joined the Navy. As luck would have it, his first stateside duty
in Rhode Island put him in the same unit where Peg's brother,
Fred Griffin, was an officer. It wasn't long before Fred also
noticed something amiss with Arthur.

After visiting her brother at his base, Peg wrote to B.J.,
describing that Arthur was supposed to go to dinner with her
and Fred, but he somehow lost his wallet, license, his pass card,
and $20.

> *I gave him five dollars but of course he couldn't leave*
> *the grounds and won't be able to for two weeks or*
> *more...Honest to God Bernie that kid is hopeless–he*
> *is in Fred's office down there, he and another yeoman,*
> *and they can't do a thing with him. He won't do any*
> *work, puts his head down on the desk and falls asleep*
> *– disappears from the office several times a day and*
> *Fred has to chase all over the yard to find him.*

She told B.J.,
> *that guy...doesn't belong in the Navy...if he was my*
> *brother I'd take him to the best mental doctor in*
> *Boston–that kid is getting worse instead of better as*
> *time goes on.*

Within a couple of months, Arthur McQuaid physically
attacked two other enlistees in their bunks and was shipped off
to Washington, D.C., for psychiatric evaluation. My mother
tried to keep B.J. informed of this, as did other family members,
although his family clung to the hope that Arthur's mental health

would somehow improve. Unfortunately, Arthur was diagnosed with a form of dementia, and he would spend the rest of his long life in the VA Hospital system.

DAMNED CENSORS

Both B.J. and Peg had their troubles with military censors regarding their personal correspondence.

> *Bernie darling,*
> *Your letters to me are coming through quite regularly–*
> *received another one yesterday dated March 15*
> *[1943]. I say I received a 'letter'[;] one would hardly*
> *call it that after the censor had finished with it. I have*
> *never seen such a mess–two thirds of the words were*
> *obliterated with black ink, and the second page was*
> *cut off completely a third from the bottom of it.*
>
> *I'll be darned if I can see what right they have to do*
> *that–as much as I can gather from what's left of the*
> *letter, it was purely personal in every respect. One*
> *paragraph in particular was a mess after he got*
> *through with it–the one where you spoke of dreaming*
> *of me again–and in the next paragraph you remark*
> *about the 'exceedingly sentimental paragraph' the one*
> *you had just written.*
>
> *At the end of all that, it is written in longhand 'Sorry,*
> *The Censor.'*
>
> *The jerk – guess you aren't even supposed to dream out*
> *loud according to their standards. He must be a Baptist*
> *minister or a guy with a grudge against you. Is the*
> *censor on your ship do you know or is your mail read*
> *in San Francisco before they sent it on to me?*

For his part, B.J. told Peg,
> *It's hard to write thru the censors–they cramp my style*

when I feel like letting myself go and really telling you
things.

But sometimes, it was merely a matter of not knowing what to
say. He wrote,
  I wish I could think of something more exciting to say
  than the usual things about loving you and missing
  you. Not that I don't do a great deal of both. That's the
  point. The condition is so acute there ought to be some
  special language for emphasizing it.

  Bernie,
  Am wondering where you are tonight. I shall be uneasy
  until I hear from you again. I don't worry half as much
  when I know where you are–it's the waiting for news of
  when and where you have landed that gets me down.
  ~ Peg, Feb. 10, 1943

As Peg was writing to him, B.J. was on his way to cover the
fighting in the South Pacific A year later, now in the South
Pacific, he found it increasingly difficult to put personal things
on paper.

  It isn't that I am not fairly bursting with things I should
  like to say, for indeed I am. It is only that they aren't
  things I should care to set down for the benefit of the
  censor. They shouldn't be put on paper at all, unless
  possibly in meter and rhyme, and you know what a
  bad poet I am. (Though I did write you another one,
  one night going 'up the slot' enroute to meet the Tokyo
  Express. But it was not successful, and I did not send it
  to you.)

He told her he was *now just marking time, anticipating*
returning home for that Christmas: *The only things I*
can write about these days–the only ones that seem
worth the effort–are shooting, death, destruction and
terror…It will wear off, of course.

It was sweltering in the tropics.

> *Do you know what I want to see? A snowbank 20 feet high, with the thermometer at 15 below. I want to roll in that snow, ski on it, make snowballs out of it, throw it down your neck and eat it, (the snow, not your neck– although, come to think of it ...)*

In the South Pacific, B.J. would gain a sense of what the island and naval battles were like for Americans. In a piece datelined only *"South Pacific Base, May,"* he wrote about what American doctors were no longer calling **"shell shock."**

Even 'war neurosis' is about to be abandoned as an unsatisfactory substitute.

Instead, Navy regulations now approve the terms 'combat fatigue' to describe breakdowns occurring as the result of action, and 'operational fatigue' to include those which come merely from strain and tension in routine but exacting and hazardous war jobs.

He learned this, he reported, from covering a medical staff discussion on board a U.S. hospital ship, which was treating such cases from the months-long fighting on Guadalcanal.[6]

You can take an American away from his 'high standard of living' and set him down in tropical jungles to fight Japs, but he's likely to keep on craving the small luxuries and creature comforts that are part of his heritage.

That appears as tenable a theory as any to explain why shower baths and ice cream proved the most efficacious forms

---

6   The Guadalcanal campaign, also known as the Battle of Guadalcanal and codenamed Operation Watchtower by American forces, was a military campaign fought between August 1942 and February 1943, in The Pacific theater.

of therapy administered by War Zone Navy psychiatrists to victims of war neuroses that developed under combat conditions in the Solomons.

Here, a portion of his story was sliced out by the censor's razor blade; at the end of his copy, B.J. noted that the censor had **"eliminated criticisms of shock treatment."**

Case histories cited by the doctor showed a pattern of combative young Marines, setting out with firm resolution and even desire for action, gradually being worn down by unceasing tension and unmitigated physical hardship to the point where some violent 'participating factor,' such as a close bomb hit, would render the soldier no longer able to control himself.

Upon arrival at the hospital ship, such youngsters often had the appearance of 'very old men' and behaved like 'terrified wild animals.' Sometimes they suffered from amnesia. They found speech slow and difficult. Nearly all were hypersensitive to noises, particularly the drone of plane engines.

Improvement came at once in many cases when the patients were given access to the civilized comforts of the well-stocked hospital ship. Almost all responded to the combination of shower baths and ice cream. (The miracle working effects of this combination is understandable enough to anyone in this area, but will doubtless seem unintelligible to readers at home. You don't know what it means to go without a proper bath for longer periods, or without good food, until you've tried it.)

General George S. Patton famously got into trouble for a widely publicized instance of slapping a soldier diagnosed with battle fatigue. Patton's outrage notwithstanding, the problem was widely acknowledged by the services and accepted by readers.

A <u>Manchester Union</u> story in March 1944 featured a Candia native: "William Brown victim of Nerve Shock on New Georgia" was the subhead. The main headline noted *"Candia Veteran Tells How He Got First of Six Japs"*:

> He recently arrived back in Candia, after being given CDD (certified disability discharge). Private Brown spent six months in various hospitals, recovering from nerve shock sustained in action on New Georgia island last August.

> Brown related how an artillery shell 'landed squarely in our company killing six of our men. Four of them were from my own squad. Although the hit landed 75 feet from me, I could still feel its intense heat.'

> "I felt all right that night," Brown said, "but the next day when I attempted to resume action, I just went all to pieces. That is how nerve shock affects you. There is no real injury but you become highly sensitive to any noise. Technically, my case was diagnosed as psycho-neurosis."

THE JUNGLE WAR'S COMMON MAN

An Advanced Amphibious Force Base in the Solomons, July 13 (Delayed) – There was something called "the American standard of living" – remember?

There is a standard of living – when it is not a standard of dying – here in the Equatorial Pacific. The fact is there are many standards, most of them bad.

If you are a correspondent and you jump around a bit, you get these different standards thrown at you in small, digestible doses. For people who have to stay in one place and take it, it is often not so digestible.

I was sitting in a half-dug foxhole in Rendova Plantation,

and I was the poorest of the poor. My coverall suit was mud-caked and my heavy Marine boots were soaked. (When these excellent boots get good and wet, and you keep them on for several days, they stain your feet a fine, deep tan that apparently is irremovable.)

My back ached from toting up gear and equipment from the beach. I had not shaved since I got off the poor old USS McCawley and I had no intention of remedying the defect. But by-and-by, I thought, I would venture back into the jungle, find a fresh, running brook and take a bath.

I had had no sleep for several nights, and I was wolfishly hungry. I remember stumbling back from the beach to the correspondents' tent after going without breakfast and without lunch. Jay Norman Lodge was there [an AP correspondent] and when "The old Sarge" saw me greedily munching stale crackers, he dug down into his jungle kit and brought out his precious box of Ration K, which he insisted I accept.

I spread that pork paste on a hardtack biscuit and enjoyed what seemed the finest and most delectable morsel I had tasted since last I ate home cooking, some time back in February, 1942.

Of course, I had it easy. There was a tin shelter for me to duck into when the half-hourly cloudburst came down. I did not have to stay up a palm tree trunk nor in a foxhole out in the bush fighting off Jap snipers....

There's the real fall guy of this war – and all too many of them take their falls literally and permanently – the little fellow who carries the rifle with the knife on the end of it and goes out to the front and digs out the Jap from his rathole. He is the jungle war's common man, and he gets what the common man has always gotten – at least up to now – the dirty end of the stick....

CHAPTER THREE

CLOSE CALLS

B.J. and Army Air Force pilot in suitable Aleutian gear.

*Am sending you a paper that Judy brought home from
school–I told her that I would send it to you so that
you could see how smart she was...Bye now darling,
take good care of yourself--we'll all be waiting for you.
Love and kisses from the three home guards.*
~ Peg

After receiving this note, B.J. returned the paper, telling Peg
that:

*Judy might like to show it to her class. Bet there isn't
another kid in her school who has had a piece of her
schoolwork flown over the enemy at 50 feet of altitude
and shot at by Japs,* he wrote.

Until I began writing this book, it never occurred to me that if my father had been a bit less lucky—or any more adventurous—than he was during the war, neither I nor two of my sisters, all of us post-war babies, would have seen the light of day.

He didn't talk to me about the real possibility that he could have been killed doing his job. He occasionally addressed it in his coverage, at first obliquely. He shared some experiences in his letters to my mother, but in most of those, he either glossed over the danger he repeatedly faced or used humor to make things appear less serious than they were.

At home at Christmas of 1943, B.J. was interviewed by his old paper, the <u>Morning Union</u>:

> "Asked how he felt or acted when a ship was under air attack, McQuaid passed it off lightly with the remark that 'we just hold up handkerchiefs.' And while speaking of death he said that the men on the battle fronts have a very different consideration of death than do the people on the home front. They are facing it every day and are used to the thoughts of being killed.

> "'I made a couple bombing trips to Kiska, both at low altitudes and the second time we got shot up pretty bad, but I myself wasn't hit. Our plane looked like a sieve when we got back, and half the damn control cables were shot away. The pilot caught a slug in the leg but it didn't penetrate his clothing, having been slowed down by various parts of the airplane.'" -- Oct. 15, 1942.

This incident involved Col. William Eareckson, who conceived of the low-level bombing of the Japanese in the Aleutians because the constantly overcast skies made higher altitude raids strictly hit-or-miss. Filmmaker John Huston, a lieutenant in the U.S. Army Signal Corps, came to the Alaskan front twice to make movies for the War Department. B.J. told me that he and Huston were briefly billeted together.

In his autobiography, <u>An Open Book</u>, Huston wrote:
> "There was a journalist–I think from the *Chicago Daily News*–who went with the Colonel on a mission. The plane was hit badly, and an enemy machine-gun bullet came through the instrument panel and dropped into Eareckson's lap, spent. On the way home from the target Eareckson showed it to the journalist, who got very excited.

> "I'll give you fifty dollars for that bullet, Colonel."

> "Sold," Eareckson said and turned his plane around.

> "What are you doing?" asked the journalist.

> "Going back, of course. At fifty bucks a bullet, I can't afford not to!"

Different reporters told the anecdote differently. One wrote that B.J. started his bidding at five bucks, and the B-17 pilot didn't begin turning the plane back toward the target until B.J. offered $50. Eareckson was only kidding. The plane returned to its base. B.J.'s letter to Peg didn't open with the plane being shot up. Instead, he thanked her for sending him Judy's school paper. He was returning it, he said, along with a note he had **"written while the ack-ack was still coming up on the first mission."**

He should not have been surprised when a letter from his mother told him how Judy had expressed her concern for her daddy's safety. She was staying overnight with B.J.'s mother from time to time:
> "She said one night before she went to sleep, 'Grammy they won't bomb my Daddy's ship will they?'

> "I said 'course not.' She'd been hearing about the Japs bombing the ships, etc."

And Peg also expressed concern for his safety:

For goodness sake take no more chances like you told me about, and like the ones I've been reading in the Union. The paper has been running one of your stories each day for over a week now–they are excellent and everyone is talking about the experiences you must be having up there.

She liked his picture in the paper, too,

I thought it was swell–good enough to eat in fact. You look marvelous in uniform--oh honey I wish I could hop a plane for Alaska tonight.

His wife also expressed her opinion about those who were not yet in the fight, now ten months old for the United States:

When will they ever wake up to the fact that there is a war on and we have to have men to fight it? I get so disgusted with the lot of them that I avoid the subject as much as possible, damned sissys that's all I can say for them.

A year later, in the South Pacific, B.J. told Peg of a correspondent being wounded:

We had our first serious correspondent casualty yesterday. Os White of the Sydney Telegraph was riding down from the front on [censored] when she was hit by some Jap dive-bombers. Some people got killed. Os was blown about by concussion and wound up with two broken ankles and considerably bomb-happiness. I haven't seen him yet but the doc thinks he'll be all right.[7]

---

7   Osmar White was sent home to Australia to recover. He made it back to the war by 1944, like McQuaid covering the allies' advance across France and into Germany. His account of that theater, "Conquerors' Road" was rejected by publishing houses at the time, apparently for being too critical of the Allies. It was finally published posthumously in 1990.

He continued:

> *Darling, you must have said an extra [rosary] bead*
> *or two the night before that mission, or the old*
> *man wouldn't be around anymore. Thanks. Or am I*
> *assuming too much?*
>
> *I have now given the Japs three good chances to shoot*
> *at me and they have missed each time. I figure they*
> *have struck out, and that from here on in I've got the*
> *Indian sign on them.*

During the summer of 1943, B.J. rolled several sentiments into one letter to Peg, including this:

> *It has been raining hard here this afternoon, and I've*
> *been leading a perfectly lazy life all day. It is almost*
> *snug, sitting here listening to the rain batter at my*
> *tent. I feel guilty when I think of the poor gallant devils*
> *dying up there in the New Georgia jungles to take*
> *that lousy little hunk of real estate known as Munda*
> *Airfield. On the other hand, as you may have gathered*
> *from my dispatches–if they are getting through, I've*
> *been shot at more, and with bigger calibers, in the past*
> *two or three weeks than most people get shot at in a*
> *long, active lifetime.*

He had been covering both the naval and ground assaults in the Solomon Islands. In a piece on a new Army assault force dubbed the Barracudas, datelined Rendova Island, June 30, [1943], B.J. told readers:

I landed with the main assault on the beach of Rendova inlet, a few minutes after the Barracudas got there…The Barracudas' Garands and Browning automatics were popping like Fourth of July fireworks, answering the spats of the Japs' light machine guns and rifles, which could be distinguished plainly.

Evidence of Barracuda handiwork was all over the place. I counted five Jap bodies in a ditch beside the road. One was that of an officer.

He had fallen, face to the foe, one arm outstretched, his hand clutching a beautifully ornamented Samurai sword, which he had drawn from its scabbard. It had been of no use against Browning automatics. His face was shot off and his head nearly severed from his body. All the Jap bodies I saw were similarly hit.

However, in his letter to Peg, B.J. brushed over his reporting, instead informing her of *"some really bad news."* He lost the watch she had given him as a going-away present:

It is at the bottom of Rendova Harbor, along with my Parker Pen. I had one of those gaudy gold plated wristbands on it and somehow, as I clambered elephantinely down the rope net ladder of the poor old McCawley [she was sunk several hours later] into the waiting assault boat which was to take us in to begin our capture of Rendova Island from the Japs (there weren't a hell of a lot of them there, and those that were got butchered early in the proceedings) as I clambered down–I in some manner caught the wristband in the rope. The lovely gold watch fell into the sea.

I think that was how it happened. I didn't notice its absence for a while, and in the interim I had jumped around a lot in the boat, helping the general–of all people!–down the ladder. There was a heavy swell running and the fine, sweet old gentleman wasn't used to that sort of thing. In fact he nearly got his pants wet. I rather hope that was how I lost the watch. I would feel badly about swapping it for anything less than the general.

The USS *McCawley* (*APA-4*) was an attack transport ship. It served as the flagship for Rear Admiral Richmond Kelly Turner, who commanded the first counter-invasion of the Allies against Japan in the South Pacific.

Hours after B.J. jumped into the assault craft and lost his watch, the *McCawley* was attacked by Japanese torpedo planes. A torpedo hit the engine room, killing 15 crew members. Admiral Turner transferred to another ship while salvage operations began aboard the *McCawley*. Enemy dive bombers attacked the ship later in the afternoon without success. But that evening, the ship was torpedoed again and sank within seconds. The final blow, ironically, was from friendly fire. Six U.S. PT boats reported attacking an "enemy" transport.
It was the *McCawley*.

> *I still have high hopes of getting home for Christmas*
> *but there's beginning to appear an outside chance that*
> *I'll just miss it by about a month,* B.J. wrote to Peg on
> November 6, 1943.

He was briefly back at Honolulu when he wrote this letter, bracing his wife for the possibility that he would miss a second consecutive Christmas with his family. Logistics in getting a replacement correspondent up to speed might delay his return home until early in 1944.

He explained:
> *Perhaps they [his editors] are justified, though I*
> *cannot help feeling that they are taking some very*
> *gallant and courageous risks with my health.*

B.J.'s health issues included an acute case of malaria and a persistent low-grade staph infection, such that a Navy medical officer's note to B.J. in August 1943, said it "is urgent that you return to the United States as soon as possible because of your physical condition." A multi-glandular disorder had existed since childhood, a doctor wrote that month. He believed it involved pituitary, thyroid, and adrenal glands. "Because your work during the past six months has necessitated your living in the tropics under dietary and hygienic conditions of the worst type, I strongly advise a complete change of your duties, proper rest, medical attention, and thorough study of your case," he wrote.

But CDN boss Carroll Binder advised that B.J. should check into a Pearl Harbor hospital instead of returning to the mainland "because [it] may be necessary work from there later on."

B.J. then wrote to Peg with the news:
So maybe I'm stuck, and if so the only thing that cheers me up in the slightest degree is the assurance that I'll still make what I regard as the most important anniversary of all. That, in case you've forgotten (have you forgotten?) is February 22nd, when you and I have a date to go skiing in the Pawtuckaway [NH] mountains. It will be eight years to the day since I caught you in that weak moment with your skis sticking out of a snowbank and your head out of the other, and I swear that if you hadn't given me that affirmative look–after all the years I had worked on the case–I'd have gone away and left you there and you'd have had to stay there till the snow melted, for all I cared. Thank God, it was your heart that melted, instead, which in view of its previous granite-like condition must certainly have been one of the great geological phenomena of our time.

Back in the days he was describing, young Peg Griffin didn't lack for boyfriends. She was petite and attractive: barely five feet tall with hazel eyes and black hair. Years later, my father sometimes referred to her coloring as "black Irish," insisting that she was descended from Spanish sailors marooned on the Emerald Isle after the English defeat of the Spanish Armada in 1588.

In fact, B.J. did make it home for Christmas 1943, but not before being under fire several times more and witnessing the loss of the largest American aircraft carrier in the war as a Japanese submarine's torpedoes sank it in the Gilbert Islands on November 24, 1943.

The USS *Liscome Bay* was a new Kaiser-built carrier with hundreds of personnel aboard, including an admiral, as B.J. reported:

[It] was within a short distance of my own ship, while we were standing a general quarters alert.

After the initial explosion great columns of flame towered against the dawn sky fed by what appeared to be numerous small explosions.

The terrible spectacle faded quickly and by daylight not even smudge smoke was left to show where the ship had sunk.

Soon one of our destroyers reported she was 'picking up 60 percent survivors' but whether she meant 60 percent of the ship's personnel or that the destroyer herself had facilities to rescue only 60 percent of those in the water was not immediately clear. Other destroyers were send [sent] to assist.

It seemed incredible that any Liscome Bay people could survive so violent an explosion.

The death toll was staggering. According to the Naval History and Heritage Command website, the ship sank in just 23 minutes. 644 men were lost, including Rear Admiral Henry M. Mullinnix and 39 pilots sitting in their cockpits on deck waiting to be launched. Also lost was Ship's Cook Third Class Doris "Dore" Miller, a Black sailor who had been awarded the Navy

Cross[8] for heroism on board the battleship West Virginia during the attack on Pearl Harbor.

Among more than 200 survivors was Captain John G. Crommelin, Jr. A U.S. Navy history entry about the attack notes: "In the shower when the torpedo hit...[Crommelin] wore nothing but soap suds and suffered severe burns as he abandoned ship."[9]

A Manchester Union headline on one of B.J.'s stories datelined November 21, 1943, undoubtedly caught Peg's eye. The main headline featured U.S. Marine Corps Col. James Roosevelt, one of the President's sons. And the sub-headline was about B.J. It read: *"Correspondent eye-witness of close shave from bomb."*

The President's oldest son cheated death twice that day as U.S. forces invaded the Makin atoll[10] as part of their Gilbert Islands push. An Army regimental commander leading the assault was killed instantly when a sniper's bullet struck him between the eyes. Col. Roosevelt was within a few feet of the commander.

---

8   The Navy Cross is the Navy's second-highest military decoration awarded for sailors and Marines who distinguish themselves for extraordinary heroism in combat with an armed enemy force.

9   Crommelin was one of five brothers serving as Navy officers during the war. Post-war, he would rise to the rank of Rear Admiral and figure in the so-called "Revolt of the Admirals" in which several Navy brass opposed President Harry S. Truman's combining of the armed services under joint command. B.J. supported the admirals in an editorial in the New Hampshire Sunday News, much to the chagrin of owner and publisher William Loeb.

10   Makin is an atoll, or chain of islands, located in the Pacific Ocean nation of Kiribati. It is the largest of the Gilbert Islands.

The second near-miss happened later that day. McQuaid wrote:
I witnessed Roosevelt's second close shave this afternoon from a distance of a couple of hundred feet. This came about when one of our low-flying bombers misjudged its target angle and released a daisy-cutter bomb prematurely...

I was with a party from a warship which had come ashore on an inspection trip and we had just finished talking with Roosevelt who had then jumped aboard a jeep and set off with brother officers for the trip to our most forward positions.

Seconds later a plane swung over us and let go its deadly cargo. A giant bomb struck scarcely 100 yards ahead of our own party and seemingly at the very place on the road where we had last seen Roosevelt's jeep. The force of the huge explosion jolted the ground beneath our feet, but again Roosevelt–though within 50 feet or so of the actual bomb– miraculously escaped injury.

B.J. noted that while young Roosevelt was **laughed at once as a 'feather merchant' Marine...nobody laughs at him now. He has learned about the war the hard way, and high ranking superiors of the amphibious command respect him on his own merits as a smart, tough, hard working and experienced soldier.**

Colonel Roosevelt would receive the Silver Star for his valor during the Makin assault. In a separate story, B.J. reported on the jungle fighting on the atoll.

We jumped off the truck and ran forward through the palm trees along the beach. Hundreds of our troops were crouched behind the trees and the clumps of jungle foliage all around us. The sound of chattering machine guns, carbines and M-1s was incessant and deafening.

A mere hundred yards away, on the other side of a tank trap, a full-fledged battle appeared to be raging with half a dozen of our light tanks firing broadsides into a heavy growth of palm trees up ahead and hundreds of our troops darting forward among shell pits, palm trees and clumps of bushes. A small but efficient force of Jap snipers was said to be the object of this attack and nearly a dozen were reported knocked out while we watched the battle.

Along with our two naval aviators–Capt. Harold B. Salada of Williamsport, Pa, and Comd. Fred Reeder of Laurel, Miss. I remained in the area about an hour. Bullets whistled over and around us and frequently came uncomfortably close ...

It was a busy period for B.J. Just days after witnessing the carrier sinking and the Makin assault, he found himself 100 miles south, reporting on the aftermath of one of the Marines' bloodiest battles of the war.

Aboard an LST off Tarawa November Twenty-Five [1943]— One of the last places you'd expect to find an LST is sitting out here on the fringe of Betio's reef where there has raged during the past several days the red hottest little scrap of this whole global war.[11]

But LST's, whose initials are variously alleged to stand for Large Slow Target, Last Stop Tokyo, and Let's Sink Together, have the habit of showing up in places where no sane sailor would expect to be found and this bunch, like a group which met us up at Makin on the morning of our arrival there, has been sitting here ever since the red dawn of Dee-day.

They all showed up on schedule which surprised everybody including them. It is well they did, for they carried tens of thousands of tons of vital munitions and supplies as well as

---

11   Betio is a town on the Tarawa atoll.

indispensable items, beaching and landing gear which aided troops to establish their beachheads.

While hell was popping from the beach, including considerable medium artillery that hadn't been knocked out from our bombardment, they moved right in on Betio and commenced their unloading operations.

The reef presented a nasty problem and prevented LSTs from accomplishing the usual feat of running right up to the island command post.

(There is a great old wheeze about an LST that ran so far inland on Guadalcanal that the skipper got a court summons for colliding with a jeep and parking on the strong side of the highway.)

But the handicap was overcome in large measure when Captain Bob Bolton, commodore of this LST squadron, discovered that a bulldozer could dig a big enough bite out of the edge of a reef to permit ships to lay down ramps on the reef itself. After that it was simply a matter of driving trucks over the reef through shallow water to the land.

B.J. had known Bolton when the latter was executive officer on the USS cruiser *Nashville* (the ship on which pilot Lucky Larson had served) in the Aleutian campaign. B.J. told readers that Bolton and Captain Grayson Birch Carter were "**typical of a breed of officers–a true bulldog breed–which the Navy has put in command of its LST squadrons.**"

I had the good fortune to be in the immediate vicinity when Carter uttered the famous ejaculation, now a universal catchword in the Pacific, which is believed by many fighting men to rank with the best remarks ever tossed off in the heat of battle by John Paul Jones, Farragut, Perry or Dewey.

The commodore was standing on his LSTs wheelhouse when suddenly, without warning, twelve Jap dive-bombers peeled through clouds over Rendova mountain and headed straight for our 'flagship.'

Nobody could imagine the slightest possibility those devils would miss us (thank goodness they somehow did).

As they streaked down from the mountains, roaring like all hell, Capt. Carter was heard to announce in loud, firm, albeit rueful accents: 'Oh (censored)! This is it!'

The uncensored version makes a perfect rhyme and is closer to reflecting the average fighting man's sentiments in such a moment than the florid speeches one finds in history books.

In addition to brains and guts a successful LST commodore needs above all a sense [of] humor. Bolton, like Carter, has that in abundance. Before I turned in last night on his transom he entertained me with a fine new collection of LST yarns developed out of present operations. Many of his crew and officers including some of the skippers were the greenest landlubbers a few short weeks ago.

Once during the voyage out here half the ships in the group made an abrupt emergency turn because they mistook a shooting star for a rocket signal.

A lookout reported an enemy weather balloon floating high overhead one day. It turned out to be Venus.

On one occasion the flotilla was menaced by a Jap sub and a destroyer escort dropped depth charges. One of the skippers, who had never before experienced such a thing, felt shock from the charges in the water and excitedly reported his craft had struck a rock.

The biggest thrill came during the height of Battle Betio [Tarawa] when one of the LSTs captured a prisoner! This Jap had crawled unobserved out to the edge of the reef and was starting the long swim toward Tokyo when LST sailors spotted him. They put out one of their boats, hauled in the bedraggled Jap and after taking him on a proud exhibition tour around the other LSTs, turned him over to the Marines.

Another highlight was when Marines had to call on LSTs for an American flag to raise over conquered Betio. The Marines had forgotten to bring one with them. Captain Bolton broke out a fine new flag and presented it with LST compliments.

It was a big one—even bigger than the Union Jack which was run up at the same time and had been brought along by a British Colonial official.

Incidentally, the flag raising ceremony was interrupted at one point by the amazing apparition of a fully uniformed Jap bugler who stepped forward at the appropriate moment and began to furnish the requisite field music. General Julian Smith uttered to me startled profanity and called halt while it was ascertained that the bugler was no Jap but one of our own Marines who had lost all his clothes coming ashore in the attack and had to help himself to the habiliments [clothes] of the first dead Jap he saw that was his size.

In his book, Tarawa: The Story of a Battle, Robert Sherrod of Time-Life, references B.J.: "Three dead Japs lie in a pillbox behind the seawall. Near one of them, there is a green-covered bound volume of the National Geographic for September-December, 1931, with markings in Japanese on the ends. The first article in the volume is about New Hampshire. Says New Hampshire-born Barney McQuaid, sticking the volume under his arm, 'I am not ordinarily a souvenir-hunter, but, gentlemen, this is my souvenir.'"

B.J. showed me the volume during one of his storytelling evenings. He asked me if I could guess why a Japanese officer was lugging such a heavy book around the South Seas. When I said I didn't know, he told me, "Simple. After they took Tarawa, they were going to take Portsmouth and this guy wanted to read up on New Hampshire."

I still have the book.

UTAH BEACH

B.J.'s close calls continued in Europe. He landed on Utah Beach on D-Day Plus One, June 7, 1944. At the time, he was allowed to identify the location only as *On the Western Assault Beach.* He came in on a Higgins boat[12] with other correspondents. Next to them was a minesweeper.[13]

When a small ship hits a large mine she disappears completely from view for a few seconds in a towering geyser of smoke and waterspout. It's probably during this interval that those of her people who are blown over the side get tossed into the air, so that from a small boat only a few hundred feet away you do not see them at all.

You do not see them until the whole upheaval of water and smoke and debris subsides and then they are bobbing in water all around you and those who are left alive are imploring you, with beckoning gestures of their lifted hands and arms and with shouted pleas that you cannot hear above the wash of the sea and the noise of your motor, to come and get them.

---

12   The landing craft, vehicle, personnel (LCVP) or Higgins boat was a landing craft used extensively by the Allied forces in amphibious landings in World War II.
13   U.S. Navy minesweepers are relatively small naval warships designed to counter the threat of sea mines. They have two primary purposes in naval warfare. The first is to clear waterways of mines to protect the nation's warships.

Our Higgins boat and a motor torpedo boat which also witnessed the blast and hurried to the scene picked up nearly all the victims who appeared to be still alive.
One or two who appeared dead were picked up by a motor whaleboat and another small ship in the immediate area.

The ship which struck the mine was herself a minesweeper which appeared nearly as large as a Destroyer Escort.

The explosion had broken the back of the minesweeper.
It seemed, B.J. wrote, a matter of a split-second choice whether she would finish her process of breaking completely in two or would blow up with another terrific explosion:

One is human enough in such circumstances to start weighing the value of one's own skin against the lives of people crowding the foc'sle and fantail to get away from the terrific heat of the fire.

Having picked up survivors from the water you feel your job is done and you feel a trifle resentful against the orders issued by a young Naval officer in the boat to go alongside and stand by to take people off.

Yet at the same time you admire this adherence to the finest traditions of the sea and feel that if you do get it it will be in the best of possible causes.

Nevertheless I was distinctly unhappy while we spent a few seconds directly under her fantail, our own boat enveloped by choking fumes and smoke.

It seemed certain she would blow up at any moment and her fantail was crammed full of depth charges which were so near we could touch them and would certainly blow us all to kingdom come.

But the smoke and flame subsided, and the minesweeper became just a crippled slowly sinking ship, not much of a menace to anyone.

B.J. explained he wanted to get the name of the ship's damage control officer who did such a fine job:

But we had no time to inquire even for names of the survivors in our own boat who were with great difficulty hoisted aboard a second minesweeper. The channel sea was extremely rough and we were tossed up and down on ten foot swells.

I am afraid the survivors, most of whom appeared to have suffered some internal blast injuries, may have been painfully hurt as we struggled to lift them up rope nets toward the waiting arms of the minesweeper crew but it was the only way to get them quickly needed medical attention.

...The six survivors we picked up owe their lives to the typical amphibious small boat crew and their ability to handle craft in violent seas.

He didn't get the names of those rescued, but B.J. named the three crewmen manning his Higgins boat. They were Elmer L. Nichols, 19, of Ellenboro West Va., motor machinist mate third class; Billy Scoggin, 18, of Charleston, Miss., seaman first class; and Denver Robinson, of Hemlock, North Carolina, 20, seaman second class.

All had been in service for less than a year, and this was their first combat operation. The officer in charge of their boat was Lt. John Tripson, a former football player for both Mississippi State and the Detroit Lions.

B.J. wrote: **Their unhesitating willingness to jeopardize their own lives to rescue brothers in distress is typical of the Coast Guard and Navy tradition.**

In one of several pieces he filed on that busy June 7, B.J. told of moving up the beach to interview French civilians living nearby.

When will any of us forget the look in the blue eyes of the towheaded four year old who, her mother said, had slept soundly with her eight month old baby sister through most of the early air bombardment to waken only when a naval shell tore through the roof of the ancient stone farmhouse?

... as for the war correspondents, at least, they begin to lose it themselves after they have ardently embraced French loam a few times in avoidance of desultory .88 fire, exploding mines, low flying Luftwaffe strafers and a sharp air bombing or two.

At the end of a separate piece that day, he told readers that despite the relative calm, bullets were still flying.

This evening we took a heavy air pounding when some German bombers managed to slip in by our fighter guard. Earlier I was strafed as closely and scared as fervently by low flying German fighters as I ever have been in my life... But I am willing to take engineers' word for it that this has been a quiet day. The boss of these engineers incidentally is a Chicago boy–Lt. Col. Robert D. May.

Two days after his story about visiting the French near the beach, he described it to readers as both a "**little stunt**" and "**not very bright.**"

Some of our soldiers are being knocked off by German snipers in those same farmhouses and it's become necessary for military authorities to issue orders against military and naval personnel fraternizing with French civilians.

I suppose it's natural that people whom Nazis permitted to

remain in this coastal invasion area should be civilians upon whom they felt able to rely all with whom I have talked were ardent in professing fealty to DeGaulle and the allies.

Later that summer, B.J.'s instincts saved him from being taken prisoner by the Germans, a fate that befell three fellow U.S. correspondents. All three would survive, but two spent the rest of the war in prisoner-of-war camps.

He told readers, **It may be of some interest–it was of paramount interest to me personally–that on the day they were seized this correspondent set out for the same general area and escaped a similar fate only by the margin of a cautious hunch which caused me to stop and make inquiries about road conditions.**

The American Third and Seventh Armies were rolling across France so quickly that not only did some of their units outrace their main forces, but so did the correspondents hungry for news. John Mecklin of the <u>Chicago Sun</u>, Edward W. Beattie of United Press, and Wright Bryan of the <u>Atlanta Journal</u> heard that 20,000 German troops would be surrendering that day. The correspondents went to be there. Mecklin, a 1935 Dartmouth College graduate, said later that he expected it to be "Almost a pleasure trip–a good story without the risks of visiting the front lines."

As their Army driver slowed for debris in the road, the correspondents realized something was amiss. Driver Jimmy Schwab put the jeep into reverse, but enemy troops opened fire. Bryan was hit in the leg. The others were uninjured, but all were taken prisoner.

B.J. told his readers that he and his driver, **"Lt. Bill Harrover of Palo Alto, California, left camp a few minutes behind the Beattie party."** Their destination was the same.

But along the way, B.J. stopped to ask for directions:

A Frenchman told me Chaumont was still in Nazi hands. Consequently, when we had proceeded a little beyond Joinville and noticed a decided dearth of military traffic, I decided to try to get definite information before proceeding. We got it from nearby headquarters of a tank destroyer battalion which had been stalled in that area by the breakdown of some of its vehicles.

Its commander said every report from the south indicated Chaumont was still strongly held, probably by about five thousand Germans, and advised us to go all the way west to Troyes before turning south to Chatillion [the supposed site of the surrender].

We took the advice and were subsequently grateful even though it required overnight stop at Troyes, where we were warned by military police that even the road via Chatillon Dijohn was not yet open and that a party of correspondents who had attempted to get through the previous day had been turned back by warnings of the maqui.

As it happened, he wrote, **We found when we got to Chatillon that no one there had heard anything about the supposed surrender of twenty thousand Germans, which actually took place four days later at another point.**

Earlier that summer, as American forces began to figure out and overcome the problem of the ancient hedgerows the enemy was using to slow the U.S. advance, B.J. reported on those firefights, often at close range:

La Haye du Puits July tenth–We pushed on through the town and down the road to Lessay against the very sound advice of a public relations conducting officer and as soon as we got over the brow of the hill machine gun slugs sang along the tops of the hedges and we realized how right he was and how wrong we were.

But by then it was too late to do anything about it.
Sergeant Louis French, twenty six, of San Francisco saw
our indecision and left his protective shelter in the ditch to
grab me by the arm and haul me over behind an armored
reconnaissance car where both of us crouched as the tank
fifty feet ahead of us began to answer the machine gun
fire with its seventy five millimeter and the sergeant very
patiently explained to me what the war was about.

Having been thus educated, B.J. went about his job of getting
names of those involved in the fight: **After all, when you quite**
accidentally got this close to what was probably at this
moment the most forward active combatant tank on the
entire French front it seemed a pity not to go and get the
crews' names.

But Louis restrained him, explaining that the only way to get to
the tank would be to crawl up the ditch, which also wasn't safe
because the ditches were not yet cleared of mines.

As if to prove his point, who should show up then but
Corporal Amos Stanley, 20, of Woodbridge, Va., in charge
of mine clearing detail and equipped with the customary
broomlike mine detector. Another figure crept up from
behind a recon jeep just in back of us and greeted me with
a toothy and completely unconcerned grin. It was Private
Jesse Strickland, 24, of Carroll, Va.

Jesse noticed my hand tremble a little as I jotted names in
my notebook. 'Take it easy,' he said, 'there's not really much
danger out here in the middle of the road behind the tanks.
I doubt that machine gun will fire much longer anyhow,
though that was a bad raking they gave us as you fellows
came up.'

Young Strickland explained that he was a reconnaissance
jeep driver working in collaboration with the cub airplane
artillery spotters, several of which were putt-putting

beneath the low overcast overhead and even as he described the nature of his job shell screams began piercing the sky loud enough to be heard plainly above the din of the tank seventy-fives.

...Jesse was as unconcerned by the shell screams as by everything else going on. 'Hell, in my job a man can't worry,' he said. 'You've just got to learn to take things as they come,' and the tank sergeant nodded his emphatic agreement. The machine gun had not opened up again so we decided it was safe to withdraw a bit from this uncomfortable position at the ultimate front.

And, B.J. told readers, **We got the tank commander's name– 26-year-old New Mexican by the name of Lt. Pete Bove.**

B.J. often looked for sidebars to his main stories. One dealt with one of those spotter planes:

AN ARTILLERY FIRE DIRECTION CENTER
IN LAHAYE DUPUIS SECTOR

–These cub plane artillery spotters can get in all kinds of trouble and usually do. One who was flying quite aways behind Jerry's lines the other day had something new happen to him.

A pack of Messerschmits came up and started chasing him. This cub pilot took customary evasive action of getting down close to the ground and wheeling in circles so the Luftwaffe boys would have difficulty shooting at him.

To what must have been his considerable dismay they didn't shoot at all. They just kept pressing in on him from all directions, driving him closer and closer towards the ground until finally they forced him to land in a small field on their side of the lines.

Our side found out about this a day later when they discovered – don't ask me how because that's a little secret between me and battery counter-intelligence -- that the Germans were using our own cub to attempt to draw our artillery fire on our own lines.

The trick was a cute one even if it didn't work and Jerry will need lots of cute tricks to make up for what our artillery people say is a desperate shortage of artillery and ammunition on his own team.

Sometimes, B.J. shared lighter stories with me, too. This is one I've always liked:

Shortly after D-Day, B.J. and other correspondents were bedded down one night in a French farm field. Awakened by noise from outside their tent, B.J. heard two soldiers on guard duty.

"Hey," one said to the other, according to B.J.'s account, "do you smell that?"

"Yeah," said his colleague, "what do you think it is?"

"It's gas! It's got to be! Quick, put on your gas mask!"

Both men did so. B.J. heard nothing but silence for a minute or two, he said, and then one of the soldiers spoke.

"Shouldn't we wake them up?" one asked, referring to the correspondents. "Naw, fuck 'em!" said the other.

Curious and perhaps a bit concerned, B.J. said he went outside to investigate for himself. He felt relieved almost immediately as he caught the scent of new mown hay, something a boy from Candia would easily recognize but which two guards from Chicago had probably never smelled before.

During the Battle of the Bulge in the winter of 1944-45, the surprise German attacks led to tightened U.S. security along the tangled front lines. Rumors ran rampant about German SS troops disguised as American G.I.s attempting to infiltrate American lines and stir confusion. In fact, some did just that.

There were even reports that the celebrated Otto Skorzeny,[14] who had pulled off the escape of Benito Mussolini, held captive in Italy, was headed to Paris to kill Supreme Allied Commander-in-Chief Eisenhower. With tightened security, password checks and challenges were being enforced, as B.J. and another correspondent discovered.

Trying to figure out the extent of the German advance, they had been out in the field for a couple of days when they were challenged at a checkpoint.

"Halt! What's the password?" an Army sergeant demanded.

B.J. told him, "Look, Mack, we've been out on the road for days. We don't know the password."

The sergeant insisted. No password, no pass.

"Can you give us a hint?" B.J. said he asked.

"Well, it's something you drink in the morning."

"Orange juice?" B.J. ventured.

"No, no! It's something hot!"

"Tea?" B.J.'s colleague guessed.

---

14   Otto Skorzeny was an Austrian-born German military officer in the Waffen-SS during World War II. During the war, he was involved in several operations, including the removal from power of Hungarian Regent Miklós Horthy and the Gran Sasso raid which freed Mussolini from Allied captivity.

"No, no!" said the sergeant. "It's something you have with cream and sugar!"

"Coffee!" guessed B.J., to which the smiling sergeant said, "Pass, friend!"

"What happened then?" I would ask my father.

"Simple," he replied. "We went to Paris and assassinated Eisenhower."

Meanwhile, my mother kept sending him the news from home:
It happened up on High Street, near the Hooksett line–
plane from Grenier Field of course.

I fully expect to find one perched on our barn roof
some morning–they drive me nuts the way they zoom
around all hours of the night and day. This is the third
crash in two weeks in our vicinity.

One was in Kingston and that guy died and the other
was in Auburn and that guy scratched his chin and
that's all. He'll probably get it next time all right.

This is from an undated portion of a letter from Peg to B.J., circa 1942. Grenier Field was a U.S. Army Air Corps base in Manchester. Civilian-controlled before the war, it would return to that status post-war. It is now the Manchester-Boston Regional Airport.

GEN. JAMES GAVIN AND THE 82ND AIRBORNE

Cherbourg Peninsula, June 18 –The 82nd Airborne Division – what's left of it – was taking it easy today. All they were doing, after 12 straight days of herculean combat, was holding the most vulnerable and vital flank on the peninsula.

...For a change, the 82nd aren't doing this job alone. They

are now fighting shoulder to shoulder with their equally heroic brothers in arms, the 101st Airborne. Though they prefer to fight beside other paratroopers and glider troops, the 82nd will gladly accept help from whomsoever it comes.

On D-Day a battleship pulled them out of one tight spot up in St. Mere Eglise. On D-Day plus three, when they had nothing but a fingernail hold left on their hard-won bridgeheads across the Merderet, a battery of Long Toms miraculously appeared from the westernmost assault beachhead. "Murder on the Merderet" is what the paratroopers say they committed with those 155s against the hapless Krauts whose machine guns from the west bank of the river northeast of St.. Mere Eglise had been slaughtering the division's bridgehead reinforcement and supply echelons.

…Until today I have refrained from writing much about the 82nd because, though everyone is aware in some measure of the magnificent performance they have turned in, they have been jumping around so fast it has been impossible to determine just what they are up to at any given moment. But today, fortunate chance brought me to the command post of Brig. Gen. James M. Gavin, the division's assistant commander, who jumped with the first paratroopers up around St. Mere Eglise several hours before H-Hour and has consistently directed the division's operations ever since.

I found the 37-year-old Gavin, who is proud of the fact that he was a buck private in the ranks before he went to West Point, precariously ensconced in what is left of the village post office here, which is little more than a couple of roofless stone walls and some loose plaster.

It will be supererogation on the part of the censors if they cut out this revelation of the location of Gavin's command post, because at no time since this operation started has he maintained such a thing in any one place longer than 24 hours and it is wholly improbable that he will be in this one by tomorrow at this time.

…The slim, grey-eyed young general, whose home is Mount Carmel, Pa, still looks more youthful than his 37 years and despite visible evidence of his physical exertions of the last fortnight his voice is full of enthusiasm for "these magnificent kids" of his as he summarized their exploits since H-minus four hours.

You know about the fog we had to jump through? Well, it was pea soup, and a thousand feet high.

…These Normandy hedges are terrible things – much thicker and more widespread than we expected and we were shot at from behind every hedge and had a rough time reassembling.

…Casualties? Yes, I heard somebody say on the radio they were light. Hell. Ten percent are still unaccounted for in the original jumping. Some were killed on the beaches, I suppose. Others drowned in the seat. You never know what happens to them. Light casualties?

We have got 1300 left out of 2,000 in the 505th [regiment] . Their officer casualties were terrible. They lost most of their company commanders – their captains and lieutenants. We have had 19 majors and colonels killed.

CHAPTER FOUR

PARIS

B.J. in U.S. Army war correspondent uniform.

IN LATE JULY 1944, on the road to the liberation of Paris a few weeks hence, B.J. again had luck on his side when he and correspondent Marcel Wallenstein of the <u>Kansas City Star</u> spent an eerie night in a hotel in the newly liberated French town of Montargis. Wallenstein recounted the story later in the year in a piece in his paper after he bumped into B.J. while covering the Ninth Army's push on Germany.

"You were nearer to having your throat cut that night in Montargis than you may ever be again," he quoted B.J.

"Do you remember that creepy hotel, where we couldn't light even a flashlight, and the man who led us through the dark to a room?" Wallenstein remembered.

They had entered the town with a patrol of the 35th Infantry Division and were received "with flowers and cognac by a hysterical population. That night a family gave a feast for the patrol, some Nebraska men, inviting McQuaid and me."

The party ended, and the two went off through pouring rain and darkened streets, and they hammered for a long time on the doors of a hotel before a man they couldn't see let them in As Wallenstein recalled it "[he] told us on no condition to light any kind of a light as he had no blackout. We felt our way along a series of passages, stumbling in a darkness that was almost a solid thing. We followed our guide up two flights of stairs, he opened a door, cautioned us on no account to show a light, and left us."

The next morning, Wallenstein wrote, "There was a curious emptiness about the hotel, and the feeling both of us had experienced the night before remained in the morning light.

"It was a feeling that is difficult to describe, a subtle warning that can neither be seen nor heard but is felt by men living close to danger. We had both spoken of it the night before, remarking that the hotel and the room and the man who showed us the way all had a disturbing quality impossible to define. I remember McQuaid saying, 'A man could disappear in a place like this and never be found.'"

As B.J. related it to his friend months later, and Wallenstein recounted to his readers, "I went back there soon afterwards. The hotel where we spent the night was full of Germans. They must have been hiding there when we took the town. That fellow who showed us our room probably was a German. Remember how he insisted that we must not light a match? It would have been simple to have killed us both and rolled us into that canal. The day we left, thirty Germans came out of the hotel and surrendered."

It was another of the late-night stories my father would recount while sitting with his Scotch and Lucky Strikes in his living room. That one still gives me chills.

B.J. covered the liberation of Paris that summer. It was a joyous but still dangerous few days in which German snipers were active. Charles De Gaulle, leader of the Free French Forces, was shot at during a ceremony at the Cathedral of Notre Dame. CDN correspondent Helen Kirkpatrick was there and had to duck for cover beneath a church pew.

Of the march into the heart of the city, radio correspondent Paul Manning of the Mutual Broadcasting System wrote, "It is hard to place on paper what really happened in Paris that Friday. The city was like a champagne dream."

Correspondent Ernie Pyle is reputed to have looked down from a hotel balcony at the wild, joyous, drunken crowds in the street and said, "Any G.I. who doesn't get laid tonight is a sissy."

B.J. reported it this way:
PARIS August 25 – We came in in our jeep through the Gate of Orleans, on a southern approach to the city, at midafternoon, about four hours after the first spearheads of General Phillipe LeClerc's French armored division had penetrated the town via the same route.

We had run completely off our map at the suburb of Montrouge and after that we just drove more or less blindly toward what we though [sic] must be center city.

Our progress was constantly impeded by thousands of liberated Parisians, delirious with the joy of their new freedom, who stormed out from sidewalks and threw themselves across streets in front of us. It was exactly like the entry into any other freshly liberated French town, except that Paris is a big city, and our welcome was bigger and noisier. There was little evidence that so-called 'battle of Paris' had been a tough fight. In all, I counted only five

of LeClerc's tanks–all light tanks–knocked out between the city limits and the Hotel de Ville.

Germans had evidently put up only token resistance, and shortly after our arrival Gen. Von [sic] Choltitz, commander of the Paris garrison, signed terms which amounted to unconditional surrender. As we approached the bank of the Seine, French G.I.s standing beside stalled tank columns joined ordinary citizens in warning us that hard fighting still raged on the opposite bank of the river from which we could hear the furious chatter of machine guns and occasional sound of shell bursts.

We stopped at a district police station to check this and were told there was fighting not only on the opposite side of the river but in the nearby Senate and Chamber of Deputies, whence there indeed issued noise of a good deal of shooting. But when we drove down to the river bank, and crossed it near the Cathedral of Notre Dame, we found it as quiet as the side from which we had come. In terms of street fighting I saw at St. Malo and elsewhere, the 'battle of Paris' was a very dull show.

But, he wrote, there was still danger and death:
This doesn't mean there has been no fighting here. The Parisian equivalent of the Maquis, led by an element of the Paris police force, seems to have been carrying on vigorous guerilla war with the Germans for more than a week.

Even as I write this piece in a hotel room in Place Delopera [sic], the rattle of rifle and machine gun fire rings intermittently over the roofs of the town. But it is not street fighting. It is only anti-sniper stuff, and fanatical Jerries hiding out in upper stories of various buildings will all be rounded up in a few hours.

To be sure this did not save the life of a young Maqui[15] whom I saw slain a few minutes ago as we drove down to watch 'the battle of the Senate' which consists mostly of a terrific fusillade of machine gun fire from French tanks which completely surround the area. Some last-stand Kraut lurking behind an eighth story window frame potted [shot] him right through the chest.

If you want a picture of what Paris is like today imagine Chicago or New York or any other great American city with citizens lining streets en masse cheering frantically at every new incoming jeep, mobbing the vehicles' occupants if they can possibly slow it down for a moment, the women overpowering its occupants with their hugs and kisses, and the men appearing almost equally enthusiastic with their fervent handclasps and shouts of vive LaFrance and vive la Ameriques. Imagine the city hall with its walls and cornices well-chewed by shellfire and every window sandbagged– that is the appearance presented by the Hotel de Ville. Imagine tanks lining streets at various points and at others carefully disposed with their turret guns pointed toward areas of possible counterattack. Imagine jubilant crowds still milling around in the streets as darkness begins to gather, with champagne corks popping in every cafe and restaurant while the rifles and machine guns continue to pop–but less frequently–outside.

One of the more fantastic touches of the afternoon was De Gaulle himself dashing around town in a big slinky black French limousine preceded by armored recon cars in a sort of triumphal parade. Everywhere he went he drew the same sort of terrific applause drawn by the G.I.s themselves, and liberally punctuated by machinegun [sic] fire from the sniper-infested areas.

Though LeClerc's French armored outfit spearheaded the drive on the town, they were ably assisted by the American

---

15   The term for the French underground and resistance.

Fourth Infantry Division, which came in from the south protecting the French right flank. Meanwhile, other strong elements of American infantry and armor were encircling Paris in broad sweeps from both north and south which by this hour must have completely surrounded the city.

Enthusiastic evidence of affection and gratitude which the Parisians bestowed upon their liberators were equaled by marks of their seething hatred for their erstwhile overlords of the master race. As part of his surrender agreement the Nazi garrison commander put several dozen of his officers at the disposal of American authorities to go out around town and order the various pockets of sniper resistance to lay down their arms. When people lining the streets saw these uniformed Germans riding around in jeeps they rushed them, spat on them, clawed at their faces and stripped their insignia from their uniforms. Eventually it became necessary to clothe them in French uniforms to disguise their identity.

I saw enough of the mobs' mounting fury to be sure that if this step had not been taken some of these Germans would have been torn to pieces before the day was out. The Germans themselves–and they were all of the highly self-touted officer caste–looked like the whipped and abject creatures they are, full of fear and wretchedness.

A few days later, a massive liberation parade drew an estimated one million citizens to the *Champs-Élysées*. B.J. filed 1800 words that were lovely and lyrical in the original but toned down by his Chicago editors.

Fortunately, B.J. kept his typed original. It read:

PARIS, August 28 –There have been in Paree the weekend glorious, the weekend magnifique, the weekend fantastique. It has been the weekend very gay, very sad, tres comique mais aussi tres tragique. There has been very much laughter and very much tears, very much love and very much hate, very much eating and drinking and very much hunger.

The edited version began:

Paris, Monday, Aug. 28 – Paris has had a magnificent, fantastic weekend. There has been much laughter and tears, much love and hate, much eating and drinking and much hunger.

The editors also removed B.J.'s speculation about whether Gen. De Gaulle **… was truly the popular hero and sage statesman who deserves and has earned his hour of triumph at the head of the magnificent, triumphant, enthusiastic and slightly chaotic parade (or) is he the would-be dictator who is the clever man for taking the spotlight but whose personality is too cold, too colorless, too eccentric to hold for long the affection of this affectionate, spiteful, warmhearted, cool headed, excitable, lovable, quarrelsome, eccentric, beautiful nation?**

B.J. wrote that … **it was clever to have prepared so quickly in advance of the parade…all those posters and banners which so much to the exclusion of every other consideration emphasized the name and the authority of DeGaulle. But was it so clever to have put so much emphasis on the slogan 'DeGaulle au Pouvoir' and are not perhaps the Parisians and all the French and all the people everywhere getting as fed up with that word pouvoir [can] as this correspondent has been pour long temps?**

Still, there was much for readers to take in and enjoy in the edited version of this piece. My father and his friend Wallenstein, along with their jeep driver, Pvt. Helmer Peterson of Chicago, went out early in the afternoon to secure a spot near the *Arc de Triomphe*. B.J. thought it would be a fine spot for parade watching:

It turned out to be otherwise. Within 10 seconds of our halt at the curb a considerable percentage of the thousands of people drawn up along the streets swarmed into and onto the jeep until they had not only smashed our windshield but left us little breathing room.

There must have been about 35 in our jeep. There were tattered ruffians who looked as if they had just come out from under a rock or a chapter of Victor Hugo, fresh-skinned beautiful young girls, mothers holding up their small sons and daughters to witness this historic event, a sweet-faced matron who spoke good English and turned out to be the wife of a Paris banker.

B.J.'s original draft reported that it was fathers holding up their children, not the "**several bedraggled looking filles**".

The local banker and his wife then took the two correspondents to his private club, where they found a score of men and women drinking champagne. Soon the two writers were drinking as well and chatting with their hosts:

…and at about that point the war started. There was a terrific fusillade from the street outside where numerous tanks and armored vehicles of the French second division were parked rather too closely together and somebody inside shouted that German planes were strafing overhead. Some people in the place hit the deck fast and disappeared under tables but the banker, an old soldier and a cool cucumber, kept on sipping his champagne and talking quietly and Wally [Wallenstein] and I did a fair job of maintaining our composure and we just went on with our conversation.

But the shooting kept on and bits of plaster began falling down and there was a skylight directly overhead so we moved madame over into a corner and I said I would go out to see what it was all about.

The rear entrance led me into a courtyard where I saw about half a dozen French G.I.s firing rifles rapidly and without apparent purpose at surrounding upper story windows. I tried to calm some of them down enough to tell what the shooting was about but they just gesticulated wildly as I have seen green American troops do in the jungle when

alarmed by a clump of coconuts mistaken for a Jap sniper. In the middle of this terrific blanket of fire aimed promiscuously at all sides of surrounding buildings a very engaging, slightly too plump, very French blond appeared from a fourth story window behind a small balcony in the very center of the place where most bullets were hitting and started hanging out some laundry.

The anti-snipers immediately shifted their field of fire away from her but continued to shoot in all other directions and as masonry showered down all around her she looked down and I gave her a GI wink and she gave me a terrific smile and went on hanging out her laundry.

His editors revised this anecdote as well. The woman was now "an engaging plump French girl." But they left in the sharing of winks.

The last sentence of the original piece–also cut from the published version—fortunately survived in B.J.'s draft:
On Friday as a matter of fact I was quite closely shot at myself, a couple of hours after Germans had officially surrendered and sent their officers around to tell the boys in various pockets of resistance to knock it off.

THE YOUNG NAZI

June Ninth Aboard Amphibious Force Flagship in Western Assault Beach Area Bay de La Seine.

The young Nazi lieutenant was prematurely grey and had the patient, tired look of the old soldier. His brown eyes were curiously gentle and limpid but there was something unpleasant about his smile and something worse than unpleasant about his soul.

He was every inch the Nazi, and answered my questions

with an amazing kind of cringing arrogance which I have seen in bad dogs but never before in a human being.

He said he spoke no English, which was a lie, and so Ira Wolfert whose knowledge of German is kindly called "working", served as interpreter for a group of correspondents riding on an LCT (Land Craft Tanks) taking a group of slightly wounded German prisoners out to a first aid ship.

The German said his gang had known all about our invasion plans and since May 16 had known exactly where we would hit. In that case, I inquired, why was the landing such a pushover? Oh, it was a trap, he said.

We would find out in a few days what they had prepared for us. He said Americans were smart, tough fighters but lacked tenacity, that they quit when the going was tough. This is what captured Germans say and is evidently a cardinal point of their indoctrination.

The British, he said, were neither smart nor tough. He said the war would be over in a couple of months now, but that first there would be another Dunkirk in which Anglo Americans would all be pushed back to the sea.

Germans, he said, were the world's best fighters because they had been at it so long and knew all the tricks of the trade as we would shortly find out.

We told him we hoped it would be demonstrated that Americans are the best handlers of modern triphibious weapons and machines. But he disagreed emphatically. "No," he said, "no," forgetting his boasts about Germans. The best fighters of all these days are the Russians.

They have the only answer to the machines which is to keep on coming into them. He must have known what he was talking about if he spoke truly when he said he had fought a long time in the Ukraine and Caucasus.

"Tell him," I told Ira, "That we've been in the Pacific a long time and we think on the basis of the ridiculous ease of this amphibious landing that the Japs are much tougher than the Germans."

This really hurt the Nazi lieutenant. You could tell by the way his eyes dropped and the funny look of wounded vanity that came over his face. But all he did was to shrug his shoulders.

We really felt sorry for him and desisted from our ribbing. After all, it's a little too easy to score off a war prisoner even if he is an unreconstructed Nazi.

CHAPTER FIVE

ROBERT BLOOD

Editor Robert M. Blood

I went to 'Nick' Blood's funeral last Friday afternoon with Aunt Margaret. She had been in Rhode Island, but came home early when she heard about the Bloods so called me and insisted that I should go with her.

It was very plain and simple in the Grace Episcopal Church. Quite a crowd on hand–mostly from the Union-Leader…The family requested no flowers be sent so I abided by their wishes.
~ Peg, Feb. 10, 1943

Robert McCutcheon Blood was the editor of the <u>Manchester Union</u> and <u>Manchester Leader</u> throughout the war years. A stern taskmaster, he was also a father figure to many of his staff. He would lose his own two sons to the war. U.S. Army Air Corps First Lt. Nickerson Blood died in an airplane crash in Texas in 1943. Younger son Rogers Blood, a U.S. Marine, was killed in action in the South Pacific, posthumously earning the Silver Star. The Bloods' only daughter, Betty, was an ensign with the Navy WAVES.[16]

B.J. wrote to Blood when he heard about Nick's death. He kept the editor's thank-you reply in which the father explained his son's crash.

"Being a flier yourself and [being] with these wonderful boys in the fighting lines," Blood wrote, "you will understand even better than I can what the circumstances mean."

Nick Blood was an exceptional pilot who had applied for combat service every time he got the chance but was turned down due to his value as an instructor. Having worked for several seven-day weeks, 10 hours a day, at Waco, Texas, Nick and two friends decided to fly their own planes, his father said, to get in a little practice.

It was Sunday, January 31, 1943. Nick was the lead in a very close formation, and when he went to land, his tail came into contact with the following plane, and both went into spins. The trailing plane was high enough to pull out, but Lt. Blood's plane, with a passenger aboard, could not.

Bob Blood told B.J. that one of his son's friends told him, "Nick

---

16   The WAVES (Women Accepted for Volunteer Emergency Service) was the women's branch of the U.S. Naval Reserve during World War II. It was established on July 21, 1942, by Congress and signed into law by President Roosevelt.

might have jumped and saved himself, but would not leave the man with him or his ship."

Blood got the wire late that Sunday night, "just as I was going to bed. It was one of those cold mean blowy nights such as we have been having."

Mrs. Blood was already asleep. He wrote:
"The hardest thing I have had to do was to wake up her and tell her. So you will understand why your letter touched me so deeply, and clouded up my glasses a good deal, and why I have gone into such detail about Nick's accident here, though the rest of the time we have done pretty well in keeping a cheerful face to the world, and in appreciating our blessings in view of the losses some parents have to meet. We know what happened, and Nick is home with us. We are really fortunate.

"But I have learned a lot of things in the past few weeks", he told B.J., "and most of them have done me good. But I shall make a terrible newspaper executive from now on, because never again can I judge or criticize a man or what he does."

Parenthetically, Blood added, "This is a little incoherent isn't it? But I find that is one of the penalties I am going to have to pay from now on. I know you will forgive me."

He updated B.J. on his second son, who had received his second lieutenant's bars in the Marines and had been recommended for a permanent commission.

"We hope he will get a short leave before being shipped out to where you may run across him eventually. I'm proud of him, too, he told B.J. He left Dartmouth [College] in his sophomore year to enlist in the Marines, and came up the hard way, out of Parris Island."

Bob Blood and both his sons attended Dartmouth College. Bob

was in the Class of 1906. Nick graduated in 1941. Rogers would have been in the Class of 1944.

On February 18, 1944, First Lt. Rogers Blood would lead his Company B, First Battalion, Marines platoon in a charge in open terrain against the Japanese on the Eniwetok atoll in the Marshall Islands.

With "conspicuous gallantry and intrepidity"[17] he led his men against machine gun, mortar, and rifle fire. Rogers Blood was cut down but his "heroic leadership and indomitable fighting spirit so inspired his men that they unhesitatingly pressed forward under the continuing Japanese fire and successfully routed the hostile forces." That fall, Bob Blood sent B.J. a news clipping regarding his son receiving the Silver Star. It caught up with B.J. as he switched from American to British forces in the Netherlands.

The toll of the war was showing in B.J.'s letter of reply. He wrote:

"I am glad Rogers' heroism was signalized in this way. It is not much, Bob, but it is something. Beyond this sort of thing I don't know any way at all of making up for such losses to people like you. I supposed [it] is too much to expect that these sacrifices will really sober us and mature us–as a nation, I mean–and make us more honestly and effectively intent on building a system under which this ugly business won't have to recur quite so often."

B.J. also wondered what effect all the casualties had at home.

"We get very much out of touch with the home front over here, and I suspect that for all the scores of war correspondents who dash around trying to cover this story, the home

---

17   The Silver Star is the nation's third-highest military decoration for valor in combat. It is awarded for gallantry in action against the enemy.

front's notion of what is really going on in Europe is pretty distorted. You'd be surprised, perhaps, by the scantiness of overall knowledge and understanding of the situation which it is possible to obtain even when you are right here on the ground, and manage to get round a good deal, as I do. And of course of what you do learn, you can impart but a small fraction to your readers because of censorship and red tape, most of which is probably very necessary from a security standpoint."

In his letters, even though they contained the grim news about his own sons, Bob Blood managed to update B.J. on life at the Manchester newspaper. By early 1943, the military services had taken 34 staffers. One of them, George Quimby, was in Navy training in Pensacola, Florida. A reporter-photographer at the paper, he would become a chief photographer's mate.

Two years later, Quimby was dead, the third Union-Leader employee to die in the war. Quimby fell ill aboard an aircraft carrier on its way to the Pacific theater. He was put ashore at San Diego and died in a hospital there of acute peritonitis.

"His poor mother is in the state hospital with a nervous breakdown, and perhaps just as well under the circumstances," Bob Blood wrote.

"That home boy, Bill Thornton, who you must remember as the office boy, is somewhere in India or Burma. Frank O'Neil is back with his outfit the fourth, after being wounded twice. He is infantry in Germany somewhere now." [18]

Bob Blood was carrying on, even though more and more of his staff had entered the service, and he was struggling with the new owner of the newspaper. Col. Knox had died of a heart attack two weeks after returning to Manchester for the funeral of his longtime partner, John Muehling.

18 Thornton and O'Neil would return safely, the former serving as a longtime copy editor and O'Neil as Union Leader State House Bureau Chief.

"Things go from bad to worse," Blood told B.J. "Mrs. Knox was now …around almost every day and has ideas occasionally, and I may say frequently, which are in themselves constructive and imaginative–if I have spelled that right–but quite a trial for a poor old me who is about through because of age anyway, and has a few other problems on his hands besides. Among those are a man shortage, of course, which a hard working replacement staff doesn't quite fill, though it tries. On top of that John Quirk finally had to lay off for I don't know how long to get soaked out, having been drinking too many of his meals for too long."

"Take good care of yourself," Blood ended a letter to B.J. early in 1945. "And finish off those Krauts fast. Just think what you have been missing in the Pacific!"

Mr. and Mrs. Blood and their daughter attended the launch of the USS *Rogers Blood*, a destroyer, on June 2, 1945. Mrs. Blood christened the ship in her son's name.

Bob Blood died in 1950, having stepped down as executive editor. As he had instructed, his obituary was published in the Morning Union and Evening Leader just as he had written it.

But the newspaper preceded the Page One story with a note that explained that the obituary: "…doesn't begin to do the man or his career justice, a fact that his staff knows fully and poignantly…He allowed his innate modesty to sway his news judgment. Those who knew the man well–and they were many–will realize why. 'Self' never counted with Bob Blood. He gave of himself untiringly; that is to say, he gave of himself untiringly to others–to these newspapers and other newspapers on which he had been affiliated; to the public as a whole; to his countless friends; and—very, very surely–to his beloved family.

"No news article, no other written tribute, can properly pay tribute to Robert Blood. The real story of his brilliancy in journalism, his kindness to his staff and to all other individuals, his constructive influence on this city and this state, cannot be properly told because Robert M. Blood, if he were here, would have vigorously blue-pencilled that honest and sincere evaluation."

One of those holding down the fort at the <u>Union and Leader</u> with Bob Blood was Peg's aunt, Margaret (nee Kean) Callahan. She grew up in Manchester with three sisters and a brother. Her formal education ended in the 8th grade. Married for just a month, she lost her husband to Spanish Influenza in 1919. She took a job at the newspaper and rose to become head of the accounting department and its *de facto* chief financial officer. Peg worked briefly for her, sometimes chatting with B.J., whose reporter's desk was in the adjoining newsroom.

With the war, Mrs. Callahan took on more responsibility. Newspaper co-owner Col. Knox was Secretary of the Navy. Partner Muehling was older and ailing. The associate publisher was Edmund "Ned" Jewell, who had been instrumental in helping Manchester recover from the Depression-era collapse of the mighty Amoskeag Manufacturing Company. But like Knox and others, Jewell was called to active U.S. Navy duty during the war.

The "executive suite looks like no man's land," Margaret wrote to B.J. "Commander Jewell never gets to the office, as when he gets home it is on weekends. Col. Knox hasn't been in these parts for ages...Mr. Muehling has been in Florida since December [it was now April]."

Margaret told B.J. that she expected a little activity in the executive offices, though, "as the Army and Navy are to make their headquarters here in a drive for Air Cadets. And more than 50 employees had signed up to donate blood for the Red Cross to produce lifesaving plasma. Most of the girls from the Accounting Department headed by their Chief [herself] will do their bit."

At the newspaper, Margaret wrote, advertising was in a bad slump, with Manchester having few defense industries and merchants finding it hard to get stock. Circulation, though, was unusually high "and if we hadn't gone to three cents [per copy] when we did, right now we would be taking an awful kick in the pants."

"Nicky Blood's death was a severe blow to Bob and his wife, but they have been very brave," she added. "The count was up to 41 employees taken for war service," she said.

"Art Brush who has two children has been going through the heebie jeebies[19] for the past three months. He feels morally certain that they will take him and he is scurrying around trying to get himself nicely placed, as using his own words he didn't think he would like to do latrine duty.

"I know that there must be times when you are pretty lonesome, but I also feel that you would be terribly disappointed and so would Peg if you had not done just as you have done.

"Many of the men in the newsroom are envious of you and wish they could have done something along the same line. I am sure you are wise enough to take the best possible care of yourself so that you and your little family may have happy and healthy days together in the not too far distant future. This awful war will someday come to an end, but none of us are too optimistic over that end coming in a hurry."

Margaret told B.J. that his wife was doing well in all respects: "I have to pinch myself to realize that she is the same little girl I knew ten or fifteen years ago," she wrote, telling him how Peg had handled the selling of her father's Manchester home after his sudden death.

———————

19   A common slang term in the first half of the 20th century, the "heebie jeebies" described a condition of extreme nervousness caused by fear, worry, strain, etc.

B.J.'s articles were being given featured play in the <u>Union and Leader</u> and had been read by all, she wrote, adding her voice to those calling on him to write a book.

"We are all expecting that you are laying the ground work for a book. Are we right? You're an awful sucker if you don't, " she told him.

CDN Foreign Editor Carroll Binder wrote to him on the subject in August 1943.

"Your dispatches have also attracted the attention and admiration of Bobbs Merrill [book publishers]…who publish Bob Casey's books. I cabled you their desire to sign you up for a book…"

"I explained that your duties in the field for the Chicago Daily News did not permit you to write a book at this time but that we would have no objection to your doing…As others have done, namely take a leave of absence after your return to prepare such a book."

Parenthetically, Binder told him of a "very severe blow" in "the Boss's decision not to permit publicatif a book about subs [submarines] upon which Bob [Casey] had worked hard for many, many months." The Boss mentioned was Col. Knox.

SCREWY LOUIE, MERCHANT MARINER

Undated aboard merchant marine liberty ship on the cross channel invasion run.

A seagoing correspondent gets used, after a while, to various kinds of navies. There's the destroyer Navy, the cruiser Navy, the carrier Navy, and submarine Navy. Each is different from the other – has its own way of dointhing things, its own jargon and its own philosophy, but within these separate categories are usually marked similarities. One destroyer sailor is like another destroyer sailor, for instance.

But for the moment I am in the Merchant Marine Navy, which is so far outside all the categories that I am sure it doesn't even resemble itself.

Take Screwy Louie, the bosun. Surely there aren't any more sailors like Louie, even in the Merchant Marine. How do you classify a Boston Irishman who hates Stalin and the Communists but who is inordinately proud of his record of 22 months as a company commander with the Abraham Lincoln brigade in the fight of the Spanish Loyalists against Franco?

Really there is nothing screwy about Louie – whose full name is Louis Oliver, 39, -- except for his complex political opinions and their reflections in his multi-colored seagoing past. The captain says Louie is one of the best sailors on the seven seas and is known as such in every port worldwide. Louie's own explanation for his fight against Franco is very simple: "I am a union man and hate all the Fascists because they are against union men, huh?" (Louis never makes statements. His statements are all in the form of questions, with this abrupt and challenging "huh?" on the end of all of them.)

Louie says you have to have Irishmen in any war but that really all men are pretty much the same in war. "Seventy percent of the men in my company in Spain were American Jewish boys," he says. "And I will never ask for any better fighting men than they were.

Before fighting Franco, Louie once served a five-year hitch in the U.S. Army, but outside of that he has been a strictly seagoing character since boyhood. Three ships have been sunk under him in this war and he once reached Murmansk in a convoy that had four ships left out of 35.

His experience is one reason why green youngsters fresh

from farms and factories whom you find in abundance on medium cargo ships of this type on the invasion supply run manage to handle their cranes and winches with a minimum degree of damage to expensive tonnage of highly delicate technical apparatus and a minimum number of accidents in discharging high explosives into small boats and lightering craft in these heavy channel seas.

If you want to call Louie "typical" it's all right with me, but I doubt it.

...B.J. also quoted Louie as noting that the Merchant Marine manned a ship of this size with 42 hands (as opposed to 200 on a Navy craft), plus 30 Navy men and one officer to guard the deck crew. The Navy officer was:

... an old acquaintance of mine, Lt. Harry Lippincott, 38, U.S. Navy Reserve. Maybe Harry is typical too. When I knew him he was a mild-mannered little social worker handling affairs for the Community Chest in Manchester, New Hampshire. Now that he is boss of a gun crew Harry still maintains his social consciousness but I am afraid he has lost his mild manners.

One thing that is certainly typical of all seafarers is Merchant Marine hospitality.

I suppose this is the first ship in history that ever carried such a strange cargo as 50 – count 'em 50 – war correspondents and to worsen matters this ship is not fitted to carry personnel. The best that Army conducting officers – who had not made any particular arrangements for our billeting – could suggest was that we all sleep on the bare deck in one of the holds. All too many of us are doing just that, but a fortunate minority – mostly former Pacific correspondents who can smell an empty bunk four leagues off – quickly

made individual deals to share berths of ship's officers and crew during their hours on watch.

B.J. was one of them.

CHAPTER SIX

CENSORSHIP

B.J. McQuaid and AP's Norman "The Old Sarge" Lodge, Solomons.

THE CENSORSHIP FOR American war correspondents during World War II was unlike anything before or since. During the Vietnam War, many reporters were highly critical of the U.S. government's approach in their reports, which embittered many military commanders and appalled some World War II correspondents, including B.J.

Unfettered reporting like that practiced in Vietnam and since then simply did not exist during the Second World War. The censorship was total, although applied unevenly and sometimes nonsensically. It was also exacerbated by technical delays in getting stories transmitted. Correspondents often needed explicit permission from an officer in order to speak with any military personnel.

Several of B.J.'s existing typed pieces show sentences and paragraphs edited and penciled out. Sometimes passages have been neatly cut out using a blade. There was not always time or inclination for a correspondent to debate the matter with a censor.

Different correspondents reacted differently. B.J.'s reactions may have improved things for some writers in the Pacific Theater. In Europe, they got him into hot water. And it doesn't appear that having as his publisher Col. Frank Knox, a major member of Roosevelt's War Cabinet, gained him any special favors in this regard.

The delays in getting his Aleutian Islands coverage published were the longest, in part because of the sheer length the stories had to travel. While he was one of the very few reporters in that theater, the censorship aspect was as new to him as it was to the military.

Even after the Japanese landed troops on Kiska in June 1942, the public didn't hear of it for weeks.

"Time [magazine] criticized the Navy's 'drum-tight censorship and pointed out caustically that the only news from the Aleutians was coming from Radio Tokyo. Following the same line, Life [magazine] assailed the military for its dribbles of 'hints and half-news,' and tried unsuccessfully to clear its reporters into the Alaska theatre," wrote author Brian Garfield in his book, The Thousand-Mile War.

B.J. tried his best to get his stories through. He wrote to U.S. Navy Captain Leland Lovette, who was directing public relations for Secretary Knox, on September 30, 1942:
The accompanying story, dealing with the torpedo attack on the aircraft tender Casco, mentions the fact that a Jap sub

was sunk. I fully realize this is forbidden by correspondents' regulations. But in this instance the story is such a good one that I decided, with the full consent and approval of Comtaskforce 8, to include it, in the hope that the account would be considered sufficiently useful by your department to permit its release.

It took a month for a reply: Request denied.

B.J. was told that seven of his stories had been released "after certain deletions." But Lovette rejected the submarine story, even declining to identify the "certain vessel" that had been torpedoed. Since the Navy Department had not issued a release on the matter, neither could B.J. He was also denied approval for a story dealing with Army-Navy command relationships. The only explanation given was that "the War and Navy Departments do not desire to announce these commands and relationships at this time."

But another request was granted, perhaps because B.J. played on the inter-service rivalry:

Repeatedly we notice up here the use of Navy names in copy appearing in various newspapers. This is also against my regulations. But we have a lot of Navy heroes up here. The Army is all the time using names from this area. In fact I happen to know that the War Department has asked the local Army authorities to be especially alert for Army heroes in this region, so that they can be supplied for use in Presidential radio broadcasts. Have I your permission to go ahead and use names, whenever special circumstances warrant? Then you can cut it out down there, if that seems advisable?

Lovette agreed, and he praised B.J.'s reporting. "Let me compliment you on the highly interesting stories you have sent through. They are outstanding in my opinion."

Peg was also getting news reports, although the ones from unofficial sources seemed the most accurate.

> *Jim Mahony called me the other day to tell me that a wire had just come into the office, saying that you were taking Weller's place. He said that you had landed at New Caledonia–are you going to be stationed there or will it be the mainland in Australia?*
>
> *...According to the radio last night things are getting pretty hot down that way again, but we can't believe all we hear. One commentator says one thing and the next guy will say just the opposite. I don't know which one to believe so swallow nothing. The only one I care about in this whole war is you...Don't stick your neck out, will you darling–it isn't worth it, and you'll make out just as well by playing cozy–and you won't be a coward either, take my word for it.*
> *~ Peg, April 16, 1943.*

War correspondents also had to contend with rules and regulations regarding how to get to the action–or anywhere close to it. In the Aleutian campaign, B.J. managed fairly well. In the South Pacific, it was a different and vexing story, one he laid out to CDN Foreign Editor Binder in April 1943.

Navy officials had suggested that B.J. and the other correspondents each choose a ship to join and wait for that vessel to be involved in combat. That might mean, he wrote to Binder, that he could be without any meaningful stories for weeks or months at a time. But, at least with a ship assignment, the living conditions were tolerable.

Correspondents stationed at South Pacific command headquarters often found themselves given poor accommodations, atrocious food, and a lack of respect—if not outright hostility—from some officers and enlisted sailors.

"There are so many unnecessary and unjustifiable handicaps imposed on us that it would require at least ten thousand words to enumerate them...There is nothing personal in it–though an uncomfortable number of naval officers despise newspapermen, misunderstand their motives, and are sufficiently unfamiliar with the basic principles of democratic government to misinterpret completely the function of a free press. I have nevertheless been personally well treated, by nearly everyone, up to an[d] including Admiral Halsey."

B.J. wrote to Binder from New Caledonia, where Southern Pacific Command (COMSOPAC) was based:

"Our plight is poetically sad. We are quartered at a French 'hotel.' A number of enlisted men are also quartered here. Facilities are naturally much inferior to other hotels, reserved for officers. There is a community shower and toilet and the open sewers for which Noumea is noted run right through the rickety wooden building. (This is convenient. You can dump your slops without leaving your room.) It stinks quite a bit, and the food scares me.

"If you don't want to eat here you can stand in line for an hour or two and get into the Pacific hotel–one of the better ones. However, you are apt to find that by the time the line has moved up to your spot, the dining place is closed. Many of us have given up eating as a regular proposition. We subsist on beer and spam sandwiches procured at the officers [sic] club. Yes, they admit us to the club here as members, which is at least one improvement over Pearl Harbor. One public relations officer told me and Joe Driscoll: 'Why the hell should we let you birds in? We won't even take in the master mechanics from the yard.

"The communications situation was just as "terrific," he wrote sarcastically. "We are limited to 1,500 words a day–1,500 words for the whole lot of us [he estimated about 30 reporters], not per individual. This may be somewhat extended if enough advance notice is given. Somebody in Congress or some place should investigate this 17 center per word rate which the so-called free French owners of Radio Noumea charge for deferred press. (The urgent rate is 50 cents!)."

One Navy public relations officer (Lt. Jim Bassett, "a hell of a nice kid" with whom B.J. would remain friends post-war) and one yeoman, "occupying one end of a small Quonset hut, handle the news machinery of this entire South Pacific war area. Is not this fantastic? How many Navy press agents are there, do you suppose, in the city of New York today, occupying how many square feet of floor space, and assisted by how many WAVES?

[He'd had] "a fine long chat with [Admiral William] Halsey yesterday during the course of which I congratulated him on the success of the Navy's policy of confusing the correspondents. He was not angry. He chuckled appreciatively."

B.J. sounded discouraged, recalling a CINCPAC[20] assistant chief of staff telling him, when he had first arrived at Pearl Harbor after his Aleutian coverage, "that he couldn't for the life of him understand why, under the circumstances, newspapers wasted money keeping men out here. After nearly a year in the Pacific I agree with him without reservation."

There were only three major things wrong with the news policy in the South Pacific, B.J. summed up:
Lack of air transport reduces the mobility of correspondents to the vanishing point.

Communications are lousy and expensive.

Living conditions–personal accommodations–for the correspondents are so inferior that most of them look inferior, feel inferior, do inferior work.

---

20   CINCPAC Fleet Headquarters, also known as Commander in Chief Pacific Fleet Headquarters, was located during World War II at Joint Base Pearl Harbor, Hawaii.

"There seems to be utterly no realization of the need for keeping the home population informed, and of the intimate relationship between a good press and strong and enlightened popular support of the war. In consequence the needs of the correspondents are not so much denied as merely brushed aside and disregarded, he wrote.

"Yet almost every ship you get on greets you with a demand to know why the story of what they are doing and have done in this fight isn't being adequately told!

"GOD, HOW WE'D LOVE TO TELL IT."

A few days later, B.J. told Binder of a correspondents' joint meeting with Admiral Theodore Wilkinson, second in command to Halsey. B.J.'s analysis of that meeting went to the heart of the conflict between military leaders who insisted on complete secrecy and those, like B.J. and other correspondents, who understood the need to inform the public if the public was expected to support the war.

Wilkinson told the correspondents–off the record–that Halsey was interested only in the successful prosecution of the war…

As B.J. reported to Binder:
"It was felt by some, "he said, that certain compromises must be made between the risks of giving the enemy some useful information, and the need of keeping the home front informed as to insure stout popular backing of the war effort. He could guarantee, he said, that Admiral Halsey would never under any circumstances weigh the two considerations in the same balance."

"If that meant," B.J. told Binder, "…that home front support of the Asiatic war is of no consequence beside the task of fighting the war, then I am afraid it displays a woeful defect in somebody's political sagacity.

"Moreover, whether they like it or not, compromises ARE being made, and have to be made. Everything we write should be of some interest to the enemy, and all of it, in the aggregate, must be of considerable use. I would certainly like to read a similar amount of accurate news copy about Jap Operations. The way to be certain of keeping your enemy in the dark is to keep your own people in the dark, completely and continually. The moment you consent to enlighten your own people even a little, you automatically accept the risk of enlightening the enemy."

B.J. may have been hoping that the audience for his letter to his editor would include Secretary Knox as well as the Navy censors who had to clear it before it left Noumea.

"The whole thing goes straight to a fundamental question involving the highest policy," he concluded. "I do not think such policy should be settled, under our form of government, exclusively by the military. I do not believe the American people will consent to remain completely unenlightened."

It would have made a fine editorial in 1943—or today.

Binder responded to B.J. on April 28, 1943:
"It is a matter of great regret to all of us that those who pass upon copy in your area are so much less enlightened in their attitude toward the press and the citizens, who exercise ultimate control over all American policy, than their opposite numbers in Australia, North Africa and virtually all the other theaters in which American forces are serving."

In those areas, Binder continued, correspondents are:
"…enabled to present most vivid pictures of the heroic efforts of our army and air forces. They mention the names of men distinguishing themselves, the performance of the planes, tanks and other equipment provided by American workers with most salutary effects on the morale of the families contributing the fighting men and the workers producing the equipment. I hope

that in time those who now do so much to impede the work of correspondents in your theater will see how much all who serve under them and the general war effort suffers from their inexperience in public relations and their apparent lack of trust in the integrity of the press and the good sense of the American public."

The military's handling of U.S. Army General James H. "Jimmy" Doolittle's Japan air raid, which was later celebrated in the book and movie <u>Thirty Seconds Over Tokyo</u>, didn't bode well, Binder told B.J.: "After sitting on the story for many months after the Japs had released practically everything that was to be known about it, a dozen stories including [fellow CDN correspondent Bob] Casey's, were scheduled for release on the first anniversary. Then somebody decided not to release them. The censors in North Africa, however, hadn't heard about the new timidity. Accordingly, Doolittle's stories were released over there and published here."

Binder wrote that B.J.'s earlier letter had been sent to one "who has long been interested in your work." Presumably that one person would have been Col. Knox.

In early May 1943, B.J. wrote again to Binder concerning censorship, coverage, and correspondents coexisting (or not) with the troops. The good news, B.J. said, included a plan to move correspondents living ashore into a Quonset village setting, "which houses middle-ranking staff officers, and has an excellent mess."

It wouldn't personally affect him, he wrote, "because he would soon be stationed on Admiral Turner's flagship."

"But," he continued, "it would be a blessing for other reporters: Meanwhile we are still living at the cesspool–pardon me, L'Hotel Sebastopol–and fighting off dysentery, dengue, and assorted fevers and ills."

With that improvement in view, B.J. said it was too bad that two of his fellow correspondents, one from United Press and one from International News Service, had been assaulted and beaten up by a bunch of enlisted men. As B.J. told it, the fracas may have been due in part to a case of mistaken identity and in part to the seamen's antipathy to outsiders using their late-night galley for a cup of coffee.

Correspondents had been issued a blanket invitation to use the facility. Versions of what happened differed, with the Navy men claiming that INS reporter Jack Mahon was drunk and using abusive language.

As B.J. described it:

Mahon is a fat, bespectacled refugee from the wilds of Brooklyn, who is a recent newcomer to warrior's ranks, and who, as an ex sports writer, seems more interested in the results of the Kentucky Derby than in what is going on out here in the Pacific. His attitude doesn't set so well with these tough minded military gents who have been shot at sufficiently to make them keenly aware that life is real and life is earnest.

B.J. tempered that assessment by adding that: he's not essentially a bad youngster, and will probably do all right when he 'gets the word,' which they usually do after they've ducked a little shrapnel.

The other correspondent, Bill Tyree of United Press, apparently did nothing but be there. B.J. continued, "I was at first very bitter about the thing, particularly for the sake of Tyree, who is a serious and able young man with a brilliant war record. He has been down here 15 months, been shot at a great deal, made bombing plane missions and ridden the fleet many times."

Navy brass convinced the two correspondents not to press charges. B.J. saw two morals in the tale; he wrote:

First, if the correspondents had been properly accommodated, they wouldn't have been up there in the middle of the night trying to get a handout, like tramps at the backdoor.

But secondly, B.J. said, if the two men had been wearing insignia that made them look conspicuously like officers (the rank to which they were entitled) instead of petty officer badges, he doubted they would have been set upon.

"Personally, I contribute to make my appearance as officer-like as possible," he continued, explaining that officials at Pearl Harbor had assured him that it was all right with both the Navy and the Army for him to wear Army officer devices on our hats. "But I don't know that the field manual regs have ever been changed."

Time-Life correspondent Robert Sherrod knew about censorship. In his book Tarawa: The Story of a Battle in 1944, he noted that Americans at home were not being impressed "with the hard facts of war."

Early in the war, Sherrod wrote, official "communiques gave the impression that we were bowling over the enemy every time our handful of bombers dropped a few pitiful tons from 30,000 feet. The stores accompanying the communiques gave the impression that any American could lick any twenty Japs."

Later, he said, these official releases became more matter of fact: "But the communiques, which made fairly dry reading, were rewritten by press association reporters who waited for them back at rear headquarters. The stories almost invariably came out liberally sprinkled with 'smash' and 'pound' and other 'vivid' verbs."

Such words "impressed the reading public which saw them in tall type. But they sometimes did not impress the miserable, bloody soldiers in the front lines where the action had taken place."

A sergeant gloomily observed to Sherrod that the war that was being written in the newspapers "must be a different war from the one we see."

"Sometimes," Sherrod wrote, "I thought I could see a whole generation losing its faith in the press. One night a censor showed me four different letters saying, in effect: 'I wish we could give you the story of this battle without the sugar-coating you see in the newspapers.'"

Sherrod then asked, "Whose fault was this?"
The answer, he concluded:
"[Mostly it] was not the correspondents' fault. The stories which gave false impressions were not usually the front-line stories. But the front-line stories had to be sent back from the front. They were printed somewhat later, usually on an inside page. The stories which the soldiers thought deceived their people back home were the 'flashes' of rewritten communiques, sent by reporters who were nowhere near the battle. These communique stories carrying 'vivid' verbs were the stories that got the big headlines. And the press association system willy-nilly prevented these reporters from making any evaluation of the news, from saying: 'Does this actually mean anything, and if it does, what does it mean in relation to the whole picture?'"

Australian Osmar White, the reporter whom B.J. had told Peg about when White was wounded in the South Pacific, had an insightful post-war perspective on censorship. "I think you had to be a bit of a schizophrenic to deal with the situation," he told an Australian interviewer. "Say you were in the field, and you saw your own mob getting plastered by the enemy... You couldn't tell it like it was because it would [have aided] the enemy. You had to accept the necessity for censorship in a military sense. You also, I'm afraid, had to accept censorship in a political sense."

Sherrod and White, like B.J., witnessed battles firsthand. Others relied on communiques and other second-hand information. According to author Ray Moseley, Sherrod remembered "that he had always felt contempt for 'communique commandos' who reported from rear areas and never knew 'what gunpowder actually smelled like.'"

In <u>Reporting War,</u> Moseley reports of an INS front-line reporter, Clark Lee, who rushed back to the Normandy beachhead days after witnessing the hard fighting on the Cotentin Peninsula.

Lee was told that Hank Gorrell of United Press "already had filed an exhaustive piece on it."

"Lee looked at the clean-shaven and unfatigued Gorrell and expressed doubt he had even been in Cotentin. Gorrell explained that he got this story by interviewing wounded soldiers as they were evacuated. Lee, still angry, doubled up his fists but was dissuaded from attacking his competitor."

Moseley wrote that two photographers called Gorrell "'X-ray Eyes' because they said he had a habit of writing stories with deadlines of towns the Allies had not yet quite reached."

YOU 'GOTTA BE CAREFUL'

CHERBOURG July 10 – Master Sgt. Jimmy Duval, 25 of Lexington, Ky., balanced three German seamine detonators dexterously in one hand while he lit his cigarette with the other.

"This job," he said thoughtfully, "is a good deal like milking a cow. When you are milking a cow you gotta be a little bit careful or the cow might kick you. This job is just like that. You gotta be careful."

I agreed vehemently. Duval might have been a little careless with the detonators and gotten away with it without suffering the loss of anything more serious than, say, a few fingers or perhaps an arm. But the locale of our conversation was the shambles that had once been the huge pier shed of the famous Quai Normandie and amid the steel and concrete rubble which covered the ground for an area equal to several city blocks there blossomed here and there and everywhere, like some obscene kind of ugly blossom pushing up through

the ruins, the enormous sea mines from which Jimmy and his team of Army engineers were extracting the detonators themselves.

I am sensitive to sea mines. Perhaps it is only because of my recent experience in riding minesweepers and in watching the effect these same mines produce in the vicinity of our invasion beaches when they went off under our ships. There were hundreds of them here inside the pier shed. This had apparently served the Germans as a storage shelter for the mines which they manufactured in great volume at a nearby naval arsenal.

…It was the job of Jimmy Duval and his mates to remove the mines from the rubble as part of the larger job of making this port once more fully operational.

"Is it dangerous?" said Sgt. Alex Gemmill, 29 of Sale Lake City. "How should I know? I just started in on this job this morning."

A better clue was given by Tec. Sgt. Albert W. Metzger, 35, of Elma, Washington, the tough-faced boss of a gang whose special job was to remove time clocks from the mines. He called me over to where his team was extricating the remains of a bunch of badly-banged up mines from the rubble heap and told me to listen while he reached down and fiddled with the mechanism. An ominous ticking sound issued forth.

"When you hear that," Sgt. Metzger said, "it means the mine is going off anytime between the end of the next five seconds or the next 30 days, depending on how the Jerries set them. But don't worry, I will shut if off right now," and he reached down in the rubble and made good on his promise.

You would think from the way he talked that he was a mine expert. Actually, he and all of these men were merely an ordinary service battalion of GI engineers whom the Navy had picked up and set to work on the mine clearance job.

"Hell," said William Cresselsmith, 25, of Pittsburg, Pa., ":we spent two years in England building airports. Then we came in here a few days after D-Day and they set us to work repairing roads."

"Yes," added Bernard Hagan, 23, of Conshohocken, Pa, "and we also build railroads. Last job we had was putting railroads back in shape near Carentan and down to Valognes.

"You had to be impressed with the quality of such courage as these GIs display. Perhaps after all there was little chance of one of the things going off after all the weight of explosives which had landed on the pier shed failed to explored them. But I was glad to leave after taking the names of the gang and it was only after our jeep was turned round and headed away that I noticed that directly above the gang of men working in the mine strewn rubble great sections of steel and concrete beams, broken off when the building was blown down, were swaying in the breeze, apparently suspended only by mere threads of steel piping or tubing.

...Others gave me their names .... Pvt 1st Class Henry Bandilli, 30, of Pawtucket, R.I., (the latter had just received in the mail a picture of his pretty wife and husky two-year-old son and insisted on halting all mine clearing operations long enough to show them to me. They were well worth the slight loss of time.)

...Looking back toward the ruins of the great pier shed as our jeep drove away I was reminded for some reason of a nostalgic and rather bitter piece I had read a few days earlier in which a London columnist recalled gay, lush days of the '20s when arrogantly rich American ladies (and I daresay British ladies as well) walked over these same piers from the great liners of peacetime and started on the usual tour to Paris with their lovely chins held at the proper level of indifference to the simple Normandy farmers. It would indeed be something today to see the rich ladies stepping nonchalantly through the mind-sprinkled ruins, but I daresay the casual heroism of these GI engineers is enough to compensate for any bitterness felt by either the Normandy farmers or the columnist.

CHAPTER SEVEN

PATTON

*Chicago artist, Aaron Bohrod, sketched B.J.
in Normandy, 1944.*

AFTER THE WAR, B.J. spoke highly of U.S. Third Army General George S. Patton. He twice took me to see actor George C. Scott's Oscar-winning film portrayal of Patton, whose 1944 summer dash across France and rescue of besieged U.S. forces at Bastogne that winter was legendary. My father greatly admired both the general and the actor. He also described to me how Patton spoke in a soft, high-pitched voice.

In mid-July of 1944, B.J. and other Third Army correspondents found themselves in conflict, briefly, with Patton.

Col. Charles C. Blakeney was head of psychological warfare and public relations for Third Army. In confidence, he told the correspondents about Operation Cobra, a major plan for the American forces to break out from the Normandy hedgerows where German resistance was fierce. Secrecy about that plan had been stressed in briefings to which only the most senior officers were admitted. But someone said something. Ohio University scholar and author Alexander G. Lovelace recounted the matter in an article for <u>Journalism History</u> in 2014.

As Lovelace explains it, on July 17 Gen. Omar Bradley was told that Patton himself had briefed Third Army correspondents and that they, in turn, "had informed the correspondents from the First Army who had angrily demanded why they had not been briefed." Bradley angrily telephoned Patton. Lovelace wrote that "when Patton returned Bradley's call he was just as angry. He had briefed his officers, but not the newsmen. Colonel Blakeney had told the reporters. Patton at once went to the correspondents' camp and told them how dangerous this slip was…"

Patton told the correspondents that they must understand that "both Colonel Blakeney and myself can be tried for what has happened. I am sure that none of you want to have us tried."

Lovelace wrote that Patton promised Bradley that he would fire the colonel. "However, the correspondents had anticipated this and had written out a statement exonerating Blakeney."

It was B.J. McQuaid who authored the statement, which he read aloud to Patton:
Dear Sir,
It is unanimously the opinion of the undersigned correspondents that Colonel Charles C. Blakeney of the P and PW section to which we are attached has in every respect and most admirably carried out the spirit of your news liaison policies as enunciated by you during our recent collective interview. From a news policy standpoint we find our assignment to your army under Colonel Blakeney

thoroughly profitable and richly productive of the kind of news which the people want to read and are entitled to get.

There has apparently been a most regrettable incident in which Colonel Blakeney's conscientious execution of this policy has resulted or may result in rendering him liable to official criticism.

The letter said the correspondents didn't know enough of the facts to make a judgment as to where the blame should be laid for the incident, **except it is our conviction on the basis of what we do know that Colonel Blakeney could not have been personally responsible since he was carrying out the spirit of your policy as we heard and understood it.**

If there turns out to have been any bad judgment or loose dissemination of information on the part of any of us we shall all be profoundly regretful and determined to prevent any recurrence of such incident. If this seems to be a case of interservice rivalry or bad coordination and absence of uniform policy within the service, we shall consider it equally unfortunate.

In any case, we express complete satisfaction with your policy as you have enunciated it, our admiration for Colonel Blakeney for the manner in which he has executed it, and our hope that this episode will not cause any deviation from a policy which we believe to be fundamentally sound and farsighted.

According to an official transcript of his meeting with the correspondents, Patton asked B.J. if the letter was from all Third Army correspondents. B.J. said yes, except for four who were absent covering another story.

Patton then asked that all the correspondents sign the letter and give it to him.

During the meeting, B.J. made the point to Patton that while Blakeney spoke to them, "it has not been determined whether any correspondent among us has given away any of the information given us in the briefing, or that any of us told someone else that he had been briefed."

Patton, the transcript relates, said while he trusted that this was correct, he didn't see how it could be. The evidence indicates someone talked, he said, "because I do know that other correspondents were apprised of the briefing within twelve or sixteen hours of the time you gentlemen were told."

B.J. stuck to his guns, telling Patton that First Army correspondents "were aroused because they think they are big shots and we have no business horning in. I repeat–was it established that one of us talked?"

Patton again stressed the operation was:
"…so secret, gentlemen, that no one in this Army or the First Army knows it except [for] the Chief of Staff and the Chiefs of the General and Special Staff Sections. It is necessary for them to know it so they can carry on their duties. When this information was given out Sunday morning, all the officers of the daily staff conferences, except those just mentioned, were sent out of the tent. Then the Chief of Staff, the asst. Chief of Staff, G-3, and myself, each separately, made the statement that this information must not go beyond the tent and that the officers present could not discuss it even with members of their own sections. In view of this fact, it is inexplicable to me how Col. Blakeney could have presumed to give you the information."

In fact, Blakeney had acknowledged having done so and told General Hobart Gay, Patton's chief of staff, that he realized it was a mistake on his part.

That night, Patton wrote in his diary that he didn't think the correspondents had divulged the plan to the others "but like little boys, boasted that they knew something. Then the correspondents with the First Army began to talk and found that three of their number had been secretly briefed...This anger was accentuated by the fact that there is intense rivalry between the two groups of correspondents, each group claiming that they are superior."

Col. Blakeney kept his job. Lovelace noted that "throughout the war, most of the criticism Patton received from the media came from reporters who were not attached to his Army. Andy Rooney of the Stars and Stripes was typical of this and attributed what he considered Patton's undeserved fame to: stiff competition for headlines between correspondents for the First Army and those with the newcomer Third Army, and as a result the public got a wrong impression that Patton was winning the war...A few irresponsible Third Army correspondents, looking for headlines, blew his progress full of hot air."

Lovelace noted that many Third Army correspondents, as well as Third Army historian Blair Clark, hotly disagreed with Rooney's assessment of Patton.[21]

When Patton was killed in a car-truck accident in 1945, B.J. was already back home. Hearing the news on the kitchen radio at their South Road home, he turned to Peg and said, "you live by the two-and-one-half ton truck, you die by the two-and-one-half ton truck."

"My Dear Helen,
Because you are familiar with certain aspects of the Third Army press situation which cannot at this time be fully set forth to our superiors in Chicago, and because as head of the Paris Bureau you are the primary representative of the Daily News' interests in the European theater, I am addressing this request to you.

---

21   In 1946, Clark and B.J. would join forces to co-found the *New Hampshire Sunday News*, the state's only Sunday newspaper at the time. They would be joined by two of B.J.'s brothers as staff reporters, along with Benjamin C. Bradlee, later Editor of the Washington Post.

That because of timid, inconsistent and unenlightened censorship, and because of an uncooperative, hostile attitude on the part of the public relations authority, I be reassigned as quicky as possible to another sector of the European front.

"I should prefer, and it seems to me logical in view of the present tactical situation, to be assigned to the British sector in Holland."

This letter was dated September 20, 1944, to Helen Kirkpatrick, B.J.'s CDN colleague, who was coordinating coverage from newly liberated Paris.

B.J. kept a copy, as well as the draft of another letter to Kirkpatrick dated the same day.

He referred to a "disturbing note" Helen had sent him in which, he said, he had been "charged" by unnamed officers with having used "abusive language." He denied being abusive but surmised that the claim arose "from certain animated discussions I have had with some of our censors."

There was also a suggestion that he had failed to cooperate.

"This is mumbo jumbo," B.J. wisecracked. "I occasionally get in late for breakfast. Perhaps that is what is meant."

But his real offense, he guessed:
"...has been that I have repeatedly sent service messages to Carroll Binder [head of the CDN foreign service] telling him how bad I thought this PRO [Public Relations Office] and censorship setup was, and the highly critical tone of these has infuriated the people responsible for grotesque deficiencies with which every correspondent is familiar and to which nearly all of them will testify. You yourself have run into a little of what the rest of us have had to put up with from the beginning and I should not need to expand on this point.

What alarms me most of all is that it is possible for the US Army to work in such roundabout fashion to present me, through you, with a kind of warning that I had best go along and be a good boy."

One such note to Binder was added on to the end of a feature piece he wrote just days before his note to Kirkpatrick: Message Binder Chicago please have London pressure SHAEF[22] to expedite release of three stories submitted through Seventh Army on trip to Besancon area. Stuck neck out driving nearly thousand miles of Indian country to visit southern area and then red tape restrictions held up copy.

It was his ambition, B.J. added, to outlast Hitler. He still hoped to be able to stay for climactic stories about the end of the Nazi regime, "but the combination of Hitler plus unenlightened censorship and restrictions on correspondents' mobility and freedom to employ communications outside own army area making me pretty sick."

This message is crossed out in pencil. It is unclear whether B.J. or a censor deleted it.

B.J. decided the best course was to send Helen "under separate cover, a request for my transfer from this Army to another front. If in your judgment it is better for the paper and for all of us that I run the personal risks involved in this situation and remain here, I will abide by that decision, but at least my application for transfer will be on the record. In any case it is of course my hope to return to the United States at the earliest opportunity following the collapse of organized German resistance."

The Patton-Blakeney incident was two months in the rearview mirror at this point. B.J. wondered if someone in Third Army or

22   The Supreme Headquarters Allied Expeditionary Force (SHAEF) was the headquarters of the Commander of Allied forces in northwest Europe, from late 1943 until the end of World War II.

elsewhere still harbored some resentment towards him. There is no hint of it in B.J.'s papers. But something else that he wrote may have portrayed him in a bad light.

Dated September 11, 1944, as a "memo" to a censor named Durant, it reads:
Please transmit the following to higher censoring authority with story on air supply which you are refusing transmission as of this date.

The story is refused transmission from this headquarters [Third Army] because of what is said to be a story on 'airfields' by location and purpose. This is not primarily a story about airfields but about an air operation which has already been publicly announced [Air supply of Patton's army] and about which the undersigned has already written in story which was passed.

B.J. guessed that what may have rankled the censor was his writing about the security risk of allowing civilians access to the site where air supplies were being distributed:
It would seem that the army's security consciousness might well be directed in more profitable channels.

He added that he had no objections to any cuts the censor might desire "but considers total stoppage a typical example of [a] condition which has from the beginning existed in Third Army where immaturity, indecision and timidly of censors has helped confine reporting of Third Army operations…"

The wording was nearly identical to his formal request to Kirkpatrick that he be reassigned.

While he was in the South Pacific, B.J. shared with Peg that he could only write about "shooting, death, destruction and terror." But he rarely included direct references to these in his stories. Just before transferring out of Third Army, however, he shared with readers a sobering piece about one infantry company's four-day mission. The censor toned it down.

There was "**nothing spectacular about the operation**," B.J. began the story, datelined With Third Army Forces before Metz, Sept. 19.

It was just a job 'cleaning out' some woods, routine infantry dirty work of the sort which has proven necessary on a surprisingly large scale in order to get Patton's armor across the Moselle in force.

No one can estimate just how much more of it will be required before the armor gets rolling in high gear again into and through the line of what is apparently the toughest sector of the fortified west wall.

But in order to accomplish the mission, several hundred American youngsters walked, stumbled, crept and crawled through four miles of those rain-soaked woods for four nights and days–without sleep, without medical attention for their wounded, with almost nothing to eat or drink, and under a continued hail of concentrated artillery fire as well as frequent small arms and machinegun fire from camouflaged pillbox positions.

First Lt. Doyle Royal, 23, of Washington, D.C., who came out of the experience as acting commander of his company [and the only officer left of five who began the march through the woods], told us the story a few hours after the [company] had been taken out of the line and posted on guard duty at a headquarters area in order to provide it an opportunity to rest and reorganize.

The bracketed material in the preceding sentence was eliminated by the censor as was a reference to the mission costing "fifty percent casualties in four days." The censor had also changed "company," which could number 200 men, to "unit." But he left B.J.'s reference to "several hundred American youngsters." A fifty percent casualty rate meant that half were either killed or wounded in the four-day mission.

Also censored out was B.J. telling readers that First Lt. Royal and First Lt. Dick Kimball of Oshkosh, Wisconsin, 'are believed the only two line officers in the entire division who are still on active fighting duty in France. Only a handful of their noncoms and enlisted men can claim similar records.'

Only two commissioned officers who had begun the division's campaign in France were still standing. That he was even trying to include such information may indicate how weary B.J. had grown of the cost of war.

He described how the four-day mission had:
…showed in Royal's red-rimmed eyes, and tired voice, and in his inability to remember map directions or times of day or night when the various episodes in his recital occurred. But like those of his noncoms and enlisted men who survived the expedition with him, his fighting spirit appeared completely unshaken, he displayed no trace of bitterness nor self-pity, and seemed to regard it as perfectly natural that any such outfit as his should now and again run into a situation which would [cost fifty percent causalities in four days and] require superhuman exertions and sacrifices for the accomplishment of a mission whose tactical value was incomprehensive to the men assigned to carry it out. Royal's outfit came ashore over Normandy beachhead on D plus one. His transport, the Susan B. Anthony, was mined and sunk on arrival near the beachhead and there were heavy casualties.

The censors also swapped out "heavy" and replaced it with "some" to quantify the casualties. But they left in B.J., quoting the officer, who was **…wondering for the last four days just what we had been sent into those woods for anyhow and what purpose it served. But you never know with those things. You are given a mission and you do your best to carry it out.**

And then B.J. added his own thoughts:
Doubtless you have read hundreds of such recitals since the war began. I have written dozens of them myself. Probably you are sick of reading them. I am sick of writing them and undoubtedly youngsters like Lt. Royal and his men are sick of providing material for them and would like to go home and get ready for victory celebrations which everyone seems to be preparing back in the States.

But there is another river to cross, a fortified line to go through, and after that maybe more woods to clear, and then the Rhine.
The war is not over here.

The war would not be over for another half-year.

B.J. did transfer. He was in the Netherlands just days after British Gen. Bernard Montgomery launched his ill-fated Operation Market Garden,[23] in which he planned to push through to Germany from the northern end of the Allied lines. The operation's failure to secure a strategic bridge in Arnhem was memorialized in the book and film, <u>A Bridge Too Far</u>.

JERRY IS OVER A BARREL

GRANVILLE –There are plenty of evidences of destruction by our armored columns themselves but a far greater proportion of the wrecked enemy horse-drawn and motorized transport that litters the roadsides seem to have been the victims of bombing by planes and low-flying strafers and fighter bombs. Countless enemy vehicles have been riddled from above by machine gun slugs until they

---

23   Operation Market Garden, the campaign to outflank the German defenses along the Rhine (the Westwall) and ensure a swift advance into heartland Germany, came to a sobering conclusion on 25 September 1944. With the failure to capture the bridge over the Rhine in Arnhem the operation fell short of its main objective.

are nothing but sieves. Prior to the big breakthrough the enemy did most of his moving at night, but he can't do it now. He must move by day and night, too, in his desperate effort to keep ahead of our hard-charging armor and this is duck soup to our airmen.

"We have got Jerry over the same barrel he had the French over on his race through to the sea back in 1940," a general in command of one of our most successful armored columns told me yesterday at Avranches. "This is 1940 in reverse, and if we can only keep it rolling the end will be just as swift and sure."

Meanwhile, it is pleasant to sit here on the antique veranda of a musty hotel where we stopped for an excellent lunch of beefsteak and French wine and have one's writing interrupted only by the long trains of trucks bearing German prisoners back toward the rear area from Avranches. One such train which just rumbled by consisted of 42 trucks each carrying from 40 to 60 prisoners. Most of them appeared to be Germans too – in contrast to the polyglot troops which have been opposing us in many places. Judging by their broad grins and handwaves to the local populace as they drove round a corner in front of this seaside hotel, these supermen seem extraordinarily happy with their prisoners' lot. They seemed the same way at Avranches, where to our amazement we met them coming down the town's main street in groups of anywhere from two to a dozen, completely unescorted by any of our troops and asking directions by hand signs from our MPs stationed along the route as to where they could find the nearest prisoners case.

Nurses arrive.

With Naval Amphibious Forces ashore, Western Assault area France June 10 – The First American women in France following the invasion landings came across this western beachhead today. They were a corps of Army nurses about

250 strong. I was some distance up the beach in a Higgins boat when we spotted them and we arrived at their landing point after they had been driven inland to their hospital stations in Army trucks. Like nearly everyone else who has been coming ashore here these days on LCIs the girls had to wade into shore through about 200 yards of cold water. In their case, I judged the depth to be about bust-level at the point where they flopped down from the landing craft. While they were debarking there was the usual desultory shelling of the western extremity beachhead by German 88s.

CHAPTER EIGHT

OF CIVILIANS AND A KING

B.J. with other correspondents during Operation Market Garden (B.J. being second from right.)

HE [B.J. MCQUAID] had been serving with the British on our left flank. The British treated their correspondents with deference, whisky and early morning tea in bed. The trouble was that when the batman brought tea in the morning the room, bed and correspondent might not be there. It was pretty close under the German guns.
--Marcel Wallenstein, <u>Kansas City Star</u>, Dec. 17, 1944

Many things in the European theater of World War II were "pretty close under the German guns." That included civilians as well as correspondents.

In Normandy, in a dispatch datelined "*Valognes, near Cherbourg, June 24,*" B.J. listed several of the area towns, including St-Mère-Eglise, St. Sauveur, and Montigny-le-Bretonneux.

I have seen them all–these battered, bleeding, crushed and utterly wretched towns of the invasion area–they all look the same.

Some are a little worse than the others, but only a little. Sometimes there are two houses in the block which have roofs left on them instead of one.

Our enemy the German is familiar enough with American firepower. Captured German officers have awe and dismay in their voices when they speak of American artillery.

As for the massive weight of our naval support guns, has not even Goebbels paid tribute to it in his propaganda broadcasts, blaming it for the initial success of our landing?

But that the withering destructiveness of the American artillery barrage should also make itself felt by our friends the French, and in such manner that it will scarcely be possible for them–or their children or their children's children – ever to forget it, seems something worse than grievous.

Our friends the French? Yes, I think these people of the Cotentin peninsula are our friends. At least they are not our enemies.

...It's true that some of the bombed out and shelled out Frenchmen who stand in forlorn clusters on the village street corners seem a little perfunctory in their V salutes and you will occasionally encounter a glance that's downright bitter, but I think I would be bitter if somebody backed a battleship up to my cottage and blew the roof off with a 14-inch shell even if I knew that I was being liberated in the process.

Is all this destruction necessary? In the case of the Cotentin peninsula it is, according to military men who seem conservative, fair-minded and thoroughly sympathetic to the French.

Speed was of the essence of the Peninsula campaign. It was vital to secure our supply and communications lines at the earliest possible moment. There are few good roads on the peninsula and nearly every town and city is a vital road junction or on a main highway.

To bypass these towns would not only have necessitated serious delays in clearing the area of the enemy and in opening the road to our incoming traffic but it would have meant leaving a hornet's nest of Germans on the flank of the forward movement.
In every case it was the Germans who chose to make strongpoints of these French villages and thus brought down on them the furious storms of air bombing and shelling which were the only means available for removing the obstacle to our advance in a hurry.

I see the military point all right and my mind accepts the situation readily enough, but military necessity or not it is the heart that bows down before the shocking sights–and smells–of these villages which yesterday breathed and lived and perhaps even laughed in the face of the occupier and which today are a stench in June's nostrils and a reproach to the blue skies of Normandy.

Perhaps it is just because I have not before seen any of this kind of war and am used to the comparatively civilized variety in the Pacific where you can shoot your battleships all day at a jungle full of Japs and destroy nothing more valuable than Japs and coconuts.

In the end I must fall back on the selfish but practical philosophy of a GI jeep driver who looked this town over today and said, "Now I know what some people meant back in the states when they said it was better to fight a war in the other fellow's country than in your own.

Within that story, my father told another, discounting hundreds of tales he had heard about French snipers, including women, aiding the Germans. He had run down many of them and was certain that most were the imagination of green troops:

I even had the chance to get fairly close to one episode involving a so-called French woman sniper. She was brought out from a prison stockade at the beach to a ship I was on. She had been painfully wounded by shrapnel and was taken to sick bay.

Reports ran like wildfire through the ship's company that we had one of the notorious woman snipers aboard. People began drifting down to the sick bay to fire hostile looks at her. She was a middle-age farm woman with ruddy features and strong, toil-roughened hands, looking somehow not so out of place as you would expect in this roomful of suffering, bleeding and in many cases dying men.

No one in authority knew who had sent her out to the ship or why. Her hospital tag indicated only the nature of her wounds and identified here simply as a French civilian.

Finally, a naval intelligence officer who spoke good French came to talk with her.

After a long conversation he expressed his conviction that she was an unoffending peasant who had never fired a gun in her life. She appeared, he said, to have been injured in the naval bombardment preceding our invasion and to have lost many of her friends and relatives.

She was sent on to England and I don't know what happened to her there but I think she was the basis for many of the stories that spread throughout the western assault area about French woman snipers.

A month later in the Netherlands, B.J. detailed the careless brutality of the Germans toward the civilian population there. It puts one in mind of more modern war crimes in the Russian invasion of Ukraine.

FORWARD PLATOON HEADQUARTERS OF BRITISH INFANTRY BRIGADE. BRABANDER, HOLLAND,

Oct. 18th –There are no hedgerows here and there's the wreckage of an occasional Dutch windmill–which in reality are even more picturesque than they appear on the postcards–mixed in with heart sickening debris of stout little brick homes and churches which characterize these Holland villages.

But otherwise we might as well be back in Normandy. Otherwise nothing seems to have changed.

All along the road from Oplock to Ventry you see the familiar sights, hear the familiar sounds and smell the same wretched smells. Dead men line roadsides, British as well as German, their shapeless corpses half submerged in the black Dutch mud.
Dead cattle and horses disfigured the pastures. Charred ruins of tanks and other war vehicles intrude their blackened profiles against an improbable background of autumn foliage that is as riotously multicolored in Holland as it ever is in New England or the Great Lakes region back home.

This seems no place to fight a war. But a war is being fought here. Very violent and devastating war, as wreckage of the brick farmhouses and villages show.

Overloon is a shambles. So is Brabander. And Venray, where violent street fighting is still in progress and from which we were turned back by heavy mortaring and shelling of the road.

…No destruction in Normandy is worse than what is being wrought in these hapless Dutch villages which block our approach to the Meuse river line.

…There was a huge asylum for chronic mental patients here in Brabander. It was operated by Catholic nuns and housed more than 2,000 insane women, 200 of whom were so violent they had to be kept strapped to their beds.

Not only did the Germans fail to remove these people from what they certainly knew was to be active combat zone but they deliberately neglected to mark asylum buildings with red crosses or otherwise attempt in any way to inform the allies of the character of the institution.

As an inevitable result, the place which seemed from all possible observation to be a natural strongpoint for defenders, was both shelled and subjected to air attack. The effects on the inmate population were what you would expect, and the unfortunate sisters who tried as best they could to care for these people in underground shelters during several days while the battle raged all around them had one of the roughest experiences of this or any war.

…It is doubtful if the solution to the world's ills is to meet this kind of behavior with similar savagery but no one human could fail after such experiences to read with great relish accounts appearing in news dispatches from First Army front of the destruction being wrought on German soil around Aachen."

THE KING GOES ROUND LIKE THIS
BECAUSE HE LIKES TO.

The King was George VI, the reigning monarch of the United Kingdom. B.J. reported on his visit to the Netherlands, close to Montgomery's front lines.

Muffled explosions could be heard in the distance as the King attended church services and sang hymns with several hundred British troops. No one paid any attention to the explosions.

You do not interrupt British ceremony, whether it be religious or civil, by such things as muffled explosions in the distance.
As a matter of fact today's ceremonies, which wound up the King's five-day visit to various sectors of the battle line, were simple to the point of severity.

...Attired in regulation British battle dress enlivened only by his ribbons, King George looked considerably smarter and more military than any of the soldierly bigwigs who accompanied him. And certainly much younger. I happen to have never seen the King before and was astonished by his youthful appearance. He is 48, but his color, bearing and figure are those of a much younger man.

After church, King George held an improvised investiture.

He knighted some people and gave military honors to some others. Some of the more 'enlightened' correspondents made nasty remarks about grown men, and good fighting men at that, kneeling to have their shoulders touch by the royal sword and bowing to have colored ribbons with sparking gewgaws on them hung round their leathery necks, but I take an opposite view.

These people have been doing such things to each other for centuries. It is all part of a mode of common behavior, of a set of customs, manners, and traditions which you may not wholly like but which at least are fairly predictable in any given set of circumstances and to that extent reliable.

...You'd be surprised how simple and even democratic a royal investiture in an open field in the combat zone can appear, without benefits of brass bands or court costumery and with most of the color provided by swirling leaves driven by brisk fall Holland wind and the only ceremonial music coming from the roar of Spitfire engines overhead.

The only thing that I can't figure out exactly is why the King makes these expeditions up toward the front. He is not trying to get elected to anything and has an assured postwar future.

...Of course there is home front morale to be considered but that's certainly excellent at the moment and not in any state to justify risking the King's neck.

The real explanation is probably one given to me by a member of the royal entourage who said, 'The king goes round like this because he likes to.'

...Of course all the reports are available to him at home but it is not the same thing. You don't get the same picture that way as when you get up and see for yourself.

'The King just likes to go round and see for himself.'

Sounds like the philosophy of a war correspondent.

The 82nd Airborne Division had parachuted into the Netherlands during the Market Garden operation. Members of the division spoke proudly to B.J. of their taking of the Nijmegen bridge and of their commanding officer, Brigadier General James M. Gavin. B.J. had interviewed Gavin in June about the first week of the Allies' Normandy invasion.

McQuaid described him as:
...the slim young West Pointer...whose men are proud of him because among other things 'he always jumps first from the first plane.'

His chief of staff, Col. Robert E. Wienecke of 446 Jefferson St. Glencoe, Ill., reminds you that it's [the bridge] four lanes wide and can carry any load an army can subject it to.

Every GI in the division takes time out to inform you that it's the first bridge across the Rhine any allied troops have so far secured. They are indignant at news accounts which fail to explain that the river at this point, which the Dutch call the Waal, is actually the lower and major confluence of the Rhine itself.

…Judging by the amount of fuss the Germans are putting up to deprive us of this gain, that view must be correct.

B.J. also joined up with the Airborne's 325th Glider Infantry Regiment on the last of a difficult three-day operation to clear enemy artillery from a strip of land it was using to blast away at the Nijmegen Bridge:

It was a rough deal all right. One way to estimate how rough is by means of the fact that the company which started the show with 125 effectives came out of it with 59.

As I left the Company area, some of the men had already spread thin layers of blankets on the damp floor of the forest and were starting to catch up on their lost sleep. Paratroopers aren't equipped with such niceties of warfare as tents and voluminous bedrolls. If you're still alive after one of the things these youngers had just gone through, you don't worry about the hazards of pneumonia.

JEWS AND THE DUTCH UNDERGROUND

Despite some post-war assertions that Americans were in the dark about what Hitler's regime was doing to Jews as it occurred, that is inaccurate. Jews in the United States spread the word as best they could. Frontline stories like B.J.'s in 1944 certainly made it clear to his readers:

At the beginning of the war, Holland's nine million population included about 150,000 Jews. Shortly after the German occupation Nazis began shipping these people to Poland, where they were thrown into concentration camps and most are feared to have been killed under the Nazi program of extermination.

The Nazis apparently estimated very cleverly the reaction of the tolerant Dutch populace to this ugly business, and they extradited the Jews in blocks of a few hundred at a time from this and that widely separated region, so that it was many months before the Dutch woke up to what was going on.

When they did, their reaction was characteristic. Under the guidance of the underground, Dutch citizens in this part of Holland generously offered shelter within their own private residences to their Jewish neighbors and to Jews brought by the underground from distance sections. By the beginning of 1943 every Jew in Holland except those who had married into Christian families were either in hiding or had been expatriated to Poland. Some 30,000 of them are estimated to have been saved from this latter fate by householders who took them in and either kept them out of sight altogether or successfully passed them off as visiting relatives or outright members of the family.

B.J. learned much of the Jews' story and the overall resistance, from a young couple with whom he stayed for a few days. His piece about it was datelined *With British Second Army Forces Holland, Oct. 14.*

Methods employed by Dutch underground have matched Nazi terror with Dutch cunning and with a ruthlessness which was hardly to have been expected from this naturally law abiding people.

The husband wrote for an underground publication and, after first keeping his wife in the dark for her own safety, he confided in her. She told McQuaid:

'I was all along very suspicious because he was always coming and going so secretly and at all hours. Then, just before my baby was born, they brought a Jewess to our house for shelter. Once I should have thought that I would be frightened under such circumstances especially because of the possible effect on the child, but I realized my husband was tied in very deeply with the underground and actually I was happy to be able to help him.'

'...After the liberation we learned that some of our...friends had shielded Jews and taken part in the movement.'

'...All of our priests and bishops have been anti Nazi,' the young man told me. 'And they have protested again and again the brutal treatment of the Jews. Our archbishop wrote a public letter against these practices. We have heard things from the pulpits of our churches which, if we ourselves said them aloud in the street, would cause us to be shot instantly. When the protests of our priests had no effect, many of them joined the underground themselves.'

'The Protestants and their clergy also were equally outraged by Nazi practices, and many joined the underground. If you knew the Nazis as we know them you would understand that nobody who has any truly religious principles would tolerate their brutal treatment not only of Jews but of all who go against them.'

'...They are like dogs and Hitler is their god and whatever he says they bow down to him. They kill hundreds of innocent people just because Hitler tells them to.' Her eyes filled with tears as she related how an acquaintance had been summoned to the door of his apartment one night and slain by a Gestapo tommy gun in reprisal for the murder of a German soldier in the neighborhood.

'He was a young man with all his life before him,' she said, 'and he did not even know a German soldier had been killed. These Gestapo men did not even question him or shine a light to see who it was they were butchering They just called him to the door and shot him down. How can anyone be so inhuman?'

The Nazi inhumanity was also visible at a concentration camp B.J. visited. It was in a Dutch community. He spoke of it to me in one of his late-night rambles, but I didn't know the full details of what my father had witnessed until I found the story he wrote about it.

He told me that the name of the place was pronounced "Fucked." I got the feeling that this was pretty much the fate of those imprisoned there, but I couldn't find any place name like it. In fact, as his story reported, the town's name is Vught, which sounds in the Dutch quite like what B.J. had said.

With the British forces in Vught, Holland, Friday, Oct. 27 [1944]—The bodies of 13,000 men and women were burned in the handsome, modern, scientifically designed Nazi concentration camp crematorium here, from the time of its installation in 1942 until the British advance into Holland last month.

Among those victims were 3,000 persons, butchered between D Day and the Nazi abandonment of the institution. These included 600 shot down en masse just before the SS (Elite Guards) and Gestapo men deserted for the Reich. The remaining 5,000 inmates of the camp were crammed into cattle cars and taken along. Citizens of Vught and nearby towns tried to derail these cars without success.

The figure of 13,000 is verified by the careful count kept by the Dutch civilian stokers of the camp's central heating plant, who were left behind when the Nazis fled and who are

still employed here by the Dutch Red Cross, which plans
to use the 600-acre institution, with its scores of neat, new
brick buildings and wooden barracks as a hospital and
refugee center.

The crematorium was installed seven months after the
Vught camp was established. No one knows how many were
butchered before that, nor is it possible to find out from
the many lime pits which consumed their bodies and which
are the only physically repulsive features of the camp's
beautiful institutions and grounds, set in a forest, parklike
area several kilometers from the center of this good-sized
village on Tilburg Road. Nearly all the bodies which were
fed to the crematorium were those of Hollanders, including
many Jews, but they did not all come from this camp.

So efficient did the crematorium prove–it is a sort of double-
burner affair capable of burning two bodies at a time–that
the corpses of Gestapo and SS torture and murder victims
were sent there from all Holland and sometime from as far
away as Belgium and France.

Sometimes the crematorium fodder was brought in on
the hoof, so to speak, and those living victims often were
hanged before being burned. There is a spick-and-span,
spotless, white-walled little hangman's chamber leading
right off the middle of the crematorium room. Adjoining the
crematorium room is a chamber equipped with an ersatz
marble table, on which the bodies were cut up and drained
of blood before being heaved into the fire. A thoughtful
touch is the installation of a water faucet and drain pipe for
keeping the somewhat concave surface of the table clean at
all times.

…The condition of the writer's stomach after seeing what I
already have described caused me to pass up a visit to the
torture chamber, but those who [went] were impressed by
the scientific torture gadgets, especially the well-designed
tripod-shaped instrument over which the victims were

compelled to prostrate themselves as their kidneys would break easily when they were clubbed across the small of the back.

DUTCH TREATS

With British Second Army Holland, October 15 – Was Hans Brinker the guy who shoved his fist through a hole in the dyke and saved all Holland from inundation and did he win the silver skates for it, or is that a different story altogether? Anyhow it ain't so, and in Holland they never heard of him. Never heard of the kid who stuck his fist in the dyke, I mean, and if it was Brinker they never heard of him either.

"What do Americans know about Holland?" my host asked me the other evening, he being an intellectual and erudite young man who used to be a school teacher and prominent journalist before German occupation drove him into the underground where for the last three years he has worked for the clandestine press.

"They know," I said, "that Holland has canals and windmills and a boy here who held back the sea by shoving his mitt in a dyke."

My host smiled sadly. "Ah, yes," he said, "I have heard before of this legend which is taught in the schools of America and also of England. Many of the English soldiers have told me about this boy and his dyke. It is true as you have seen that Holland has canals and windmills, and since the war we have also returned very widely to the custom of wearing wooden shoes, which had been dying out, especially in towns and cities. But this other fact you know about Holland is not true. It is not even true as legend. There is no such legend in Holland. Our own school children are not taught such nonsense as that one little boy could hold back the ocean. How is it possible in your country that such a story gains currency?"

I didn't have any answer to that one so I told him about Henry Mencken's White House bathtub, but didn't know if I got my point across." [Author Mencken invented a story about the first bathtub in the White House. It was quoted as fact for years thereafter.]

CHAPTER NINE

BATTLE OF THE BULGE

Peg (Griffin) McQuaid

WITH AMERICAN FORCES, Belgium, Dec. 19–
Although information available tonight on the depth and development of penetrations by the enemy counteroffensive is still sketchy and confused, it is more than ever apparent that Field Marshal Von Rundstedt is committing his major elements in one of the riskiest but shrewdest gambles in the history of warfare.

Depending on which way the coin falls–and it's too early to predict that–Germany will either have shot her final bolt so completely that the Allied march to Berlin should be a walkover, or will have put herself in position to prolong the struggle to a far later date than anyone heretofore cnvisioned.

In any event it is obvious that we were caught by surprise not only as to the magnitude and location of the attack but the fact it was coming at all.

It was no surprise to our leaders that Germany possessed large and powerful reserves of newly reequipped and refitted SS armored units or that she had succeeded in rebuilding a considerable air force. But I doubt that anyone had seriously estimated that she intended to employ these instruments for any other purpose than a stubborn, ground-yielding defensive of the slow yard-by-yard character.

The ultimate geographic objects of this most threatening penetration are as yet unclear.
–B.J. McQuaid

Whatever the exact dispute that caused him to request reassignment from Third Army in the fall of 1944, the move paid off splendidly. Having covered the British and Americans in the Netherlands, B.J. then moved to the U.S. Ninth Army in Belgium. On December 14, he received a note from CDN editor Hal O'Flaherty, who had taken Carroll Binder's place running the service. Addressed to B.J. at 9th Army, Belgium, the message must have pleased him: "You have full authority move at will any and all points western european zone. Stop. This also applies jack bell [a fellow CDN reporter]. Good luck."

Two days later, on December 16, Hitler ordered his forces to mount the counterattacks that would become known as the Battle of the Bulge. As the German attacks developed in the Ardennes Forest, just south of B.J.'s position, he and many correspondents were even more in the dark than Allied Command as to exactly what was happening.

But B.J. was determined to enlighten himself and his readers. He explained in a December 21 note to O'Flaherty:

Can probably reach me best by slugging messages Mackay Paris to Ninth Army via teleprinter. Stop.

Impossible use this communications base and get detailed eyewitness without cutting off self from communications for several days at a stretch. Stop.

Planning to do this over the weekend when we have long break in publication unless something big happens. Stop.

Fair overall report available here but censorship heavy. Stop.
Regards, McQuaid.

The "long break in publication" was because of Christmas. Not all American newspapers published on Christmas Day, a Monday that year. Not all had Sunday editions, either. B.J. intended to take advantage of that gap.

On Christmas Eve, B.J. found himself face-to-face with Field Marshal Bernard Montgomery. Their encounter was by sheer coincidence, he reported:

At the time we were barging about in a jeep trying to get some kind of picture of the confused melee in that area well within the pincer moves of von Rundstedt's two major drives where we were billeted with the American 7th Armored and 82nd Airborne Divisions.

Suddenly our Scottish driver explained: 'Look, there's Monty.'

It was the field marshal, all right. Accompanied by only a single aide he had just driven up before the headquarters of the American airborne divisions.

It was a 'forward area' indeed in which to encounter the commander of all the Allie[d] armies north of the German bulge. But there was Monty attired in a pair of baggy corduroy pants and familiar beret, exuding infectious confidence.

Your correspondent, summoning all his courage, waylaid the group of American generals commanding various outfits in the region when the field marshal left the headquarters in their company. Monty has a rule against exclusive interviews with the press and seemed slightly astonished at this temerity.

He asked the American generals my identity but they hadn't the faintest notion, and said so. Then he grinned and, falling into the easy attitude common at the front among American GIs and generals alike, answered my questions.

Among B.J.'s questions: **Would the Germans take Liege?**

Montgomery told your correspondent that the Germans would never reach Liege, at least not in this war.

Monty also told B.J. that the situation was excellent and it couldn't be better.

The British general's confidence was remarkable given that the outcome still seemed very much in doubt at the time.

B.J.'s next report was datelined *December 25–with American Forces in Ardennes.*

For six days this division had fought with such heroism that it disrupted Field Marshal von Rundstedt's scheme to reach Liege and Antwerp and split our armies. Armor fought armor savagely, but no less glorious was the role of the infantrymen.

With self-sacrificial heroism equaling that of the armored men, these infantrymen fought the Tiger tanks with hand grenades and M-1 rifles and held open the routes to the rear over which the armored division could be resupplied and maintained and along which it made its slow, methodical withdrawals.

I saw the last withdrawal, which was made at dusk across the Salm and Lienne rivers. All day the division had been beating off heavy counter-attacks from elite Panzer outfits on both its right and left flanks.

Counter-attacking elements themselves were able to withdraw in good order, and many of the armored infantrymen who had been left behind to cover the general withdrawal were able to straggle back across the river, rejoining their outfits during the night.

I visited one of their company command posts the following morning and found some of them still dribbling back. Typical of this kind of never-say-die fighting man was Pvt. Leo Sokolowsky, 10623 Edbrooke Ave., Chicago. He and his buddies had managed to get back with their platoon intact and complete with halftracks.

They were part of a company that dominated the important road junction of Recht, and denied enemy armor the use of it during the first crucial days of the German advance.

Nearby, B.J. found two other soldiers waiting to receive survivors from one of their platoons.

Sgt. [Michael[Lynch's analysis of the week of uninterrupted fighting was:
'There wasn't any front. There were six fronts that I have known about between St. Vith and Vielsam, and half of them were Jerry's, and we fought back and forth across all of them without ever knowing exactly whose were which.'

The Germans' two-pronged attack had created confusion
and gaps in the Allied lines, B.J. wrote. He was now with an
American armored division that had organized itself into a huge
egg-shaped position within a circle, finding itself in contact at
various points around this circle with elements of nine separate
enemy divisions.

McQuaid reported:

**It was no wonder that at high army headquarters remote
from the scene of battle correspondents gained the impression
from official reports that the division had been cut off and
destroyed. The most ominous report was that it had even
lost radio contact with the outside world. When I set out to
try to make my way to the division's area three days ago its
fate was still obscure. But I drove without difficulty to its
headquarters to learn its contacts with the rear had been
restored when a famous American infantry unit rushed to
the scene almost as quickly as the armored men themselves,
went into position directly behind it and took command of
its routes of egress leading back to the Meuse.**

At the end of his report, B.J. added his personal message,
asking that Christmas greetings be sent to his wife and family
via telegram. "Tell them," he wrote, that the greetings were
belated due to [his] having spent the last three days in combat
areas remote from communications.

Apparently lost in the scramble to cover the Battle of the Bulge
was a story request that Hal O'Flaherty had sent out a month
earlier: "As part of symposium please file week of December
18 – 23 five hundred word story on what Christmas brings to
children [in] your vicinity, their health, plans for education,
treatment of war orphans, effect of war upon them."

Two days after wishing his Christmas greetings to his family,
B.J. filed another exhaustive report telling readers more about
how American frontline forces had met the German advance:
The people who stopped him in the first crucial hours were

frontline fighting men, officers as well as lowly GIs, who paid a fearful price to stand and hold in the face of overwhelming odds against enemy armored and manpower.

I have told a small measure of the story of the American armored division which threw itself squarely athwart roads vital to rapid development of the German advance and of American infantrymen who fought Tiger tanks with hand grenades in order to keep supply routes open to armored men and protect the latter's lines of withdrawal. There was actually one period when the armored division was completely cut off except for one inadequate secondary route to the rear and when it was imminently threatened with immobility by the loss of 80,000 gallons of its gasoline and 30,000 of its food rations which enemy armored column captured in a sudden raid on its supply base.

The situation was saved by a young Captain, whose name cannot be mentioned because he has since been killed, who took his light tank company and drove across one of the main enemy routes at right angles to open a path to a giant supply base belonging to other outfits that had been caught in front of the German drive. These outfits had fled, except for odds and ends of such personnel as antiaircraft crews, military government officials, and scattered service troops.

The captain set himself up as 'mayor of Gouvy Station,' which was the name of the town and organized the loose ends of personnel whom he found there and fought off all enemy attacks for three days at the same time keeping open supply route over which vehicles of his light tank company including tanks themselves acted as supply trucks to convoy desperately needed materiel that kept his division going until it could be resupplied from more remote bases.

'There was the oddest assortment of frontline fighting troops in Gouvy Station anyone ever saw,' said Lt. John

McLaughlin of Nashua, N.H., a civil affairs officer who was himself part of the assortment.

In the same piece, he wrote of :
...The SS, full of Der Fuehrer's fanaticism, is also fighting fanatically and continues to pull every trick in the book. It drove an armored battalion out of Manhay early Christmas morning by the ruse of tailing into one of its armored columns with several of our captured tank destroyers, manned by Germans in American uniforms.

The intruding destroyers got into the heart of the village before they opened up at point-blank range on surrounding American tanks and inflicted frightful casualties. In the ensuing confusion a number of enemy tanks drove in, and our battalion, badly cut up, had to pull back its remnants some 2,000 yards. But before the afternoon of Christmas Day was over those same remnants had retaken Manhay.

The German advance, B.J. wrote, **had somewhat the appearance of a bulge.**

But it is far from a solid bulge. The stubborn islands of American resistance like that afforded by American infantry and armor in Bastogne lie athwart some of [the enemy's] main road and communications centers.

...The Germans are trying desperately to pour more men and armor supplies through this funnel to support and extend the tip but are being hammered mercilessly from the air, harried all along their flanks by local attacks from our forces assigned the mission of containing the penetration, have their main lines deep within the funnel subjected to repeated raids and blocks thrown by strong American task forces, and find their westernmost tips methodically attacked and annihilated in detail.

The situation for the enemy was so bad, B.J. reported, that

German tanks making it almost to the Meuse River had to be abandoned because their crews ran out of fuel and food.

THE MAYOR OF GOUVY STATION

IN THE ARDENNES, Belgium – Snuffy Hughes, one of the most colorful and best loved characters in the 7th Armored Division, is dead. Snuffy got it in the battle of Manhay early Christmas morning.

Censorship regulations have until now precluded mention of the casualty, or identification of Capt. Hughes as the light tank company commander who as "Mayor of Gouvy Station," resupplied an entire division with stores of the huge 1st Army dump, cut off in the first hours of Von Rundstedt's drive.

At one time the 7th Armored's magnificent effort in placing itself athwart the main routes of German advance in the St. Vith-Recht-Beho region was threatened with nullification and the division faced annihilation owing to the loss of 80,000 gallons of gasoline and 30,000 rations.

That was when Snuffy – whose rightful title was Capt. Walter J. Hughes, Surveyor, W. Va – reconstituted his famous "Blueball Express.: [that] was what he called his light tank company whenever it had to be employed as a combat train to run supplies and ammunition under heavy enemy fire to sustain other forward elements.

The Gouvy Station job, which he did only a few days before his death, was Hughes' greatest triumph. Not only did he shove his light tanks down the highways from Beho, which were supposedly controlled by powerful SS panzer forces, but he kept these routes open for three days, organized a defensive system around Gouvy and made so much noise that the Germans delayed their approach until they had

gathered immense forces to attack what seemed like a whole armored division.

By the time the Germans felt strong enough to seize Gouvy, Snuffy was gone and so were most of the supplies of the 1st Army depot. Every man in the 7th Armored was walking around with a big box of 10-in-one-ration and the name Snuffy Hughes was on every lip.

Hughes was killed when his tank ran over one of our mines, hastily laid south of Manhay as our forces, which had penetrated several thousand yards south of the village on Dec. 24, decided to pull back to Manhay and hold the line.

DON'T MESS WITH THE COOKS

WITH THE BRITISH 2D ARMORED FORCES (Dec. 18) Military cooks are like the domestic variety: when they're hurrying to get dinner ready it's a good idea not to pester them.

A two-man German patrol that infiltrated through British lines in this area a day or two ago could have saved itself considerable grief and some bad scalp wounds had its members been familiar with this simple bit of kitchen wisdom.

The cooks were two Welsh guardsmen, who had set up their company kitchen in an abandoned barn only a few hundred yards from the foremost frontline positions. They were thumping away right merrily at the mashed potatoes when they heard a gruff voice from behind them commanding in English: "Hands up."

Neither cook bothered to turn around, but one stopped whistling long enough to exclaim petulantly: "Don't pull any of your bright games on us, chum, or there'll be no supper for you tonight."

At this the "hands up" command was repeated more peremptorily, whereupon the two cooks finally turned to discover two Jerries covering them with tommy guns.

It appears that as a shortrange weapon a tommy gun in the hands of a Kraut is no match for a potato masher, which looks like a German hand grenade and is commonly known by that nickname

One cook put one Kraut out of business, while the other cook tackled the second intruder. It was all over as soon as the first cook got hold of the K.O.'d German's tommy gun and stuck it in the ribs of the Jerry rolling on the barn floor in the grip of the second cook.

The two Krauts wound up prisoners, and the cooks went on with the supper.

CHAPTER TEN

KNOX, KNIGHT

Frank Knox, U.S. Navy Secretary

DEAR BERNIE:
I have your letter of May 2 [1944] and I can appreciate what a shock it was to you to learn of the Colonel's passing.

You may not have heard, but the Colonel's trouble really started on Sunday afternoon in Manchester. He really suffered a heart attack during the course of John Muehling's funeral services. He thought it was an attack of indigestion.

…No decision has been made here with respect to the paper.
~ John [O'Keefe]

The "Colonel"–Navy Secretary Frank Knox--died of a heart attack on April 28, 1944. He was 70. O'Keefe had served Knox both as an aide in Washington and as a part-time substitute for Knox as head of the Chicago Daily News.

As O'Keefe's letter describes, Knox had returned to his Manchester home a week earlier to attend the funeral of his longtime friend and business partner, John Muehling. The two had been in business together for more than 40 years, ever since their rough-and-tumble newspaper days in Sault Ste. Marie in Michigan's Upper Peninsula.

A veteran of three wars, Knox had crossed political party lines to serve as FDR's Secretary of the Navy in the run-up to World War II. The President in a statement to news wires, said the death was a "heavy loss to us and to me especially who had come to lean on him increasingly."

"He has done much for his country; he has helped greatly in our defense and in making victory certain. Finally, I like to think of his bigness and his loyalty. Truly he put his country first. We shall greatly miss his ability and his friendship."

Knox also had been a loyal friend and a mentor to B.J. No doubt the news of his death hit hard, but there was still a war raging, and B.J. was in England preparing to cover the invasion of Europe.

Without Knox, he may not have gotten there.

While home for Christmas and for some rest and recuperation from his tropical illnesses in early 1944, B.J. was informed by his Chicago editors that, health permitting, they wanted to send him back to the Pacific, where they were short of coverage and where he had become something of an expert. B.J. protested, citing the tropical diseases and glandular fever that had laid him low. He wanted in on Europe, which everyone knew was the next big thing.

If he couldn't have Europe, B.J. explained, he would prefer the Mediterranean. As of March 4, 1944, Knox's office directed the Navy Office of Public Relations that B.J. was to be accredited to U.S. Naval Forces in northwest African waters. The PR office told B.J. it would do everything possible "to expedite your credentials and get you off to the Mediterranean without delay."

His family also thought this was where he would be headed, but on April 4, 1944, he was copied on a letter from the Navy PR office to the Commander of Northwest African Waters: "Reference Mr. Bernard John McQuaid, representing Chicago Daily News, was accredited to your command as a Navy War Correspondent. Reference is hereby cancelled, as the result of a change of plans by his newspaper."

The next day, April 5, came a letter from Knox himself.

> My dear Bernie:
> Thank you for your good letter of April 2. I got it the same day that I called you up and postponed your departure. I presume you can guess the reason for the postponement. Something else was postponed. Just what I can't tell you.
>
> What I am arranging is to have you put aboard the flagship of a cruiser division which is sailing for Europe about the middle of April. It is sailing from Boston so it will be handy for you. The Admiral commanding the task force is my old aide, Admiral Morton Deyo, and I shall make arrangements with him to take you on his flagship.
>
> I think the chances of your seeing some active service are good, and in more than one theatre.

Knox was correct: the chances were indeed good. D-Day in Normandy was just two months away. B.J. would see a lot of action over the next year—but, by then, Knox was gone. His widow held onto the Manchester newspapers for a time, but the

Chicago Daily News, with its prized foreign service, was sold to John S. Knight, owner of several large publications.

Lt. John S. Knight Slain in Nazi Ambush
By B.J. McQuaid

It must have come as a shock to B.J. Instructed by his office to check up on the son of the new owner of his news service, B.J. arrived too late. Knight's son was dead. B.J.'s story reported:

MUENSTER, Germany –First Lt. John S. Knight Jr., son of the publisher of the Daily News, was killed March 29 [1945] with three enlisted men in a German ambush at Hullern near Munster.

Lt. Knight, 22, was leading a reconnaissance party of four men during the 17th Air-Borne Division's drive on the Westphalian capital. They were two miles in front of our infantry lines.

Pfc. Earl Holcomb, 25, Fola, W. Va., the only member of the expedition to survive, said that the Germans, armed with light machine guns and grenades, held their fire until Lt. Knight's party, riding in an unarmored jeep, passed the first of their concealed positions. Then they opened fire from all sides.

'We never had a chance,' said Holcomb.

The story noted that young Knight had been married while doing parachute training at Fort Benning, Georgia, and that his wife became the mother of a son two weeks after her husband died in action. What it didn't say was that the story was not published until after the birth, lest it upset the young mother.

Lt. Knight died just a few weeks after he was awarded the Bronze Star for meritorious service against the enemy in Belgium.

At that time, with a small recon patrol, he cleared the enemy from Hautbellain, Belgium.

'In the face of a numerically superior force, the patrol, under the aggressive leadership of 1st Lt. Knight, skillfully carried out its attack completely routing the enemy,' the citation read.

Not only did B.J. have to write the story, but he also had to alert Chicago, which in turn alerted the senior Knight who was playing golf in Florida. According to his official biography, the news reached Knight on the golf course. He read the telegram and then continued with his golf game.

B.J. told me years later that he believed his being the bearer of this bad news was the reason Knight decided not to reinstate him in his pre-war job as an editorial writer in Chicago. Instead, McQuaid was told he could work for a Knight newspaper in Detroit. He told me that he had been to Detroit once and that was enough. Instead, he returned to New Hampshire.

SHOOTING AT RED CROSS GIRLS NOT GOOD IDEA, NAZIS LEARN.
By B.J. McQuaid

CDN Foreign Service Wireless
IN THE KLOTZE FOREST, Altmark, Germany, Friday, April 20—Upward of 1,000 diehard SS and Grosse Deutschland division fanatics, spearhead of a last-gasp Nazi counter-attack which before it was chopped up penetrated nearly 20 miles into the 9th Army's left flank, are being taught today that it is not a good idea to shoot at American Red Cross girls.

…Tonight in Klotze village on the edge of the forest we shall sleep peacefully and our clubmobile girls will not be disturbed by enemy raiding patrols exchanging small-arms fire with GI guards posted outside their living quarters.

It is improbable that last night's 'battle of the clubmobiles' was staged by the SS with any intent to injure the American women. It appeared purely accident that a small enemy patrol which infiltrated our forest village happened to come into contact with security guards in the Red Cross billeting area. But the fact that the girls had their slumbers interrupted by the ungentlemanly bursts of burp-gun fire at such an unseemly hour–the stroke of midnight–aroused every spark of chivalry in the neighborhood.

The girls themselves rather enjoyed the ringside seat at the moonlit show which they watched from their bedroom windows.

'I'll remember it so long as I will remember the bombing of St. Lo,' said Eloise Green, Cedarhurst, L.I. 'You could see the shadowy figures of our boys crouching in the moonlight to reload their guns, while others darted forward from one clubmobile to another returning the enemy fire.'

Most of the girls who saw the fight are veterans who have come all the way across France, Belgium, Holland and Germany, serving coffee and doughnuts to the combat troops as near the front lines as the authorities will permit them to do.

…Like our army nurses, the Red Cross girls are the darlings of the combat troops from general to buck private. They themselves have the GI philosophy and GI appearance. They are just as beaten, tired and dirty–and as game as anybody else.

One such Red Cross Girl, in snapshots my father kept in his office desk, has dark hair and a pretty smile. B.J. never talked about her to me. Some of my siblings were aware of her and her relationship with our father. My youngest sister, Peggy, doesn't recall how she knew—but she knew. She told me she once asked our father why he stayed with our mother after the war instead of "her."

"Your mother had better legs," B.J. replied.

I don't know where they met or how long the affair lasted. I found the snapshots after he died. In one, she is standing with two other women next to an American Red Cross van. In the background is a railroad car with a Red Cross insignia.

Her first name was Kay. In one picture, she is in a uniform with the Red Cross patch on her sleeve. In another, she holds her helmet in one hand. A poster behind her reads, "Their super race idea killed 25 million. We are in danger so long as that idea remains."

These women were nicknamed Donut Dollies. Might she have been one of those women that B.J. wrote about in his story of G.I. chivalry?

The pictures were in an envelope also containing a cryptic telegram sent from New York City. Dated September 29, 1949, it is addressed to my father at the Sunday News. It reads: "May be taking left for north but tongueless eels can't tell even if they love forever. [signed] Kay."

I don't know how I know this, but I think Kay became a model after the war. Speaking with my siblings while writing this book revealed no more information about her. But two of my siblings casually mentioned that our mother also had an extra-marital liaison during the war. They didn't know any details, although one sister believed the man was also from Candia.

Service message Mariano New York:
Please convey following to my wife via western union Manchester New Hampshire. Found splendid supply authentic Patou perfumes in recently liberated town and sorry no way getting them to you time for your birthday but

WAR FRONTS HOME FIRES

please take will for deed sweetheart and all my love and best wishes for happy birthday. – BJ McQuaid

This message was datelined September 6, 1944. B.J. was still with Patton's Third Army. Peg's birthday was September 9, so he was thinking ahead. Whether he was also thinking about his Donut Dolly, I don't know.

In his war trunk, he also saved a spicy one-page item entitled "Waves 1942 Model."

WAVES was an acronym for Women Accepted for Volunteer Emergency Service, a division of the Navy created during the war. According to the one-pager, the model pictured displaced 120 pounds, had an overall length of 65 inches, a beam of 26 inches, and was launched at night.

Twin mounts forward varying in caliber from 33 to 37 inches."

"Keel laid – often."

B.J. spent much of early 1945 reporting from Germany as the Allies advanced steadily into Hitler's home territory. By early April, the end was a question of when, not if, the Germans would surrender. B.J.'s stories began to focus on what would come next, noting that: **the Nazis, by what seems to have been deliberate design, have left the Allied Military Government authorities a Germany which is in a state of administrative chaos without precedent in modern times.**

He wrote of displaced persons, about expected famine in some parts of Germany, and of the mistreatment of American prisoners of war, newly freed to tell their stories.

His piece, datelined April 11 began:
With American and British Forces at the Weser [a German river, he wrote }**of one class of people in Germany whom we**

have truly liberated and how the Germans fear and dread them the hundreds of thousands of erstwhile slaves now pouring westward along every highway and country lane in the Reich.

German women, and men, too, stand in lengthening lines before newly established MP and military government posts…and demand that we do something to prevent 'these wild beasts, the Russians,' from raping their daughters and pillaging their farms. It is the Russians they complain of, never the French, Czechoslovaks, Poles, or Yugoslavs. Hitler's hate and fear propaganda against 'bolshevism' has done its work well. The Germans quake in their boots at the very name 'Russian.'

Actually, the military authorities have no evidence that the Russians are any more guilty of depredations than the other freed slaves. And in the matter of rape the Russians seem more restrained that some of the other nationalities.

Years later, in his late-night musings, my father would tell me about his encounters with surrendering German soldiers. Upon surrender, they often expressed shock and alarm that the U.S. military wasn't now going after, as they put it, the real enemy, which was Russia. He said they asked to be allowed to keep their weapons and join the U.S. to fight against the Russians.

As the Russians advanced on Berlin, Hitler killed himself in his Berlin bunker on April 30, 1945. Germany surrendered on May 8. Technically still under military command, on June 17, B.J. received orders from SHAEF[24] to "proceed on or about 28 June 1945 from London, England, to the United States,

---

24   (SHAEF) Supreme Headquarters Allied Expeditionary Force was the headquarters of the Commander of Allied forces in northwest Europe, from late 1943 until the end of World War II. U.S. General Dwight D. Eisenhower was the commander in SHAEF throughout its existence.

reporting upon arrival to the Chief, Bureau of Public Relations, Washington, D.C."

B.J. returned to the States in July. It couldn't have been a comfortable voyage, considering the vessel was an LST (built to carry tanks). But he probably didn't mind much.

He landed at Norfolk, Virginia. His trunk contained two slips of paper declaring the items he had brought back. One was the three containers of perfume, apparently those he had mentioned in his birthday greeting to Peg. The value given was $30. The second slip entitled him to retain as his property one pair of field glasses, one double-barreled shotgun, one Mauser pistol, two SS sabers, and one typewriter.

The Nazi swastika is stamped on the hilt of each saber. B.J. told me about the shotgun. Its stock is inlaid with illustrations of animals, and he found it lying next to a dead German civilian. B.J. said the man was trying to stop a U.S. tank with the weapon. The typewriter was apparently the one that he lugged around with him for much of the war. "Chicago Daily News" is stenciled on its case. A "portable," it weighs more than 13 pounds.

The war in Japan, which B.J. had first covered three years earlier, would go on for another month. B.J. didn't want to go back there. He had seen and reported on enough war. Having been told that his former Chicago Daily News job as an editorial writer wasn't open to him, and with no interest in moving to Knight's Detroit paper, B.J. went home to New Hampshire.

He told me once that Mrs. Knox, the Colonel's widow, let it be known that he could have a job as a "police reporter" for the Union and Leader. But he had been a war correspondent: he wasn't going back to being a lowly reporter. Instead, B.J. decided that Manchester and the state of New Hampshire needed another daily newspaper.[25]

---

25   Mrs. Knox apparently wasn't fond of others who had been close

He joined with Blair Clark, who had been a historian for Patton's Third Army, and Philip Weld, his friend from before the war, and the trio incorporated the name of the New Hampshire Daily News, perhaps in homage to the <u>Chicago Daily News</u>.

Clark, a scion to the Clark Thread fortune, and Weld both brought wealth to the endeavor. B.J. had none, but it was his idea, and he also had friends. One such friend was John Hammond, who had been a cub reporter with B.J. at the <u>Portland Evening News</u>. Hammond was an heir to the Vanderbilt fortune and a discerning scout of musical talent. He fashioned a long career, much of it at Columbia Records.

The small group intended to compete head-on with the <u>Union and Leader</u>, but at the last minute, Weld pulled out. Clark, B.J., and their backers (including an aunt of Ben Bradlee, who became a reporter for the new team) decided they would instead start a Sunday newspaper. There had not been one in New Hampshire since Col. Knox had tried and failed to nurse one along in the early 1920s. Back then, it couldn't compete with the big Boston newspapers.

The New Hampshire Sunday News debuted on Sunday, October 6, 1946, with Clark and B.J. as publishers. They rented office space in the former home of the Union and Leader on Hanover Street. Their offices backed up to the new Union Leader building on Amherst Street.

Back from military service, two of B.J.'s brothers, Elias and Joe, were hired as staff reporters along with Bradlee, also home from Navy service. The first issue of Manchester's new Sunday newspaper carried the scoop that William Loeb of Vermont had purchased the <u>Union and Leader</u> from Mrs. Knox.

---

to her husband. While she gave Ned Jewell the title of editor and associate publisher after Knox's death, within a year Jewell successfully sued her, claiming that Knox had promised that he would succeed the Colonel as head of the newspaper. Jewell landed at the *Washington Times* and inherited a share of that paper when Publisher Cissy Patterson died.

McQuaid and Clark didn't own a printing press, but B.J. knew the owner of the Haverhill, Mass., <u>Gazette</u>. Jack Russ was added to the new paper's board, and he allowed the new <u>Sunday News</u> to be printed on his Haverhill press, at cost, each Saturday evening. Clark and McQuaid made the drive each Saturday to the Gazette's composing room. Their product was then trucked back to New Hampshire and sold at churches and in stores on Sunday mornings, even as it began building up a list of home-delivery customers.

The <u>Sunday News</u> was scoring scoops against the <u>Union and Leader</u>. Its owners and crew were hungry to compete, and it showed. It won a national award for Elias McQuaid's work exposing a kick-back scheme between a state official and a contractor. Both men whom McQuaid exposed went to prison.

Clark and B.J., however, were not getting along. The mercurial B.J., who more than once told a staffer they wouldn't know a news story "if it bit you in the arse," was apparently causing friction. After just a year, Clark decided to exercise his option to buy out his partner. B.J., unable to match the price, was forced out.

With Peg about to have their third child, to be followed by another two in rapid succession, B.J. needed a job. An idea to start a newspaper in Dover, New Hampshire, fizzled, but then he met with Loeb and the latter's partner, Leonard Finder, at the <u>Union and Leader</u>. They let it be known that B.J. would be in charge of starting a new Sunday newspaper for them.

Clark, meanwhile, wasn't doing too well running the <u>Sunday News</u> without McQuaid. He sold out to Loeb and Finder, and they put B.J. in charge of the paper—the same one he had started two years earlier. He would oversee the <u>Sunday News</u> for the next quarter century and Loeb named him as editor-in-chief of both the daily and Sunday newspapers in 1966.

B.J. McQuaid died in April 1976. He was 67 years old. Two

years earlier, his leg had been amputated as a complication of type 1 diabetes that had been diagnosed within months of his return home from the war in 1945. B.J.'s diabetes may have been triggered by the stress of finding his place in civilian life, starting a new paper, and reuniting with his family. He had also continued to smoke heavily and drink, sometimes to excess, and tell his youngest son war stories, often late into the night in the quiet living room in his home on South Road in Candia.

Peg McQuaid lived another 14 years, enjoying her friends and her grandchildren. Also a heavy smoker, she died in July 1990 in a fire at her South Road home. It was the same home where she had coped with rationing and cold winters and cared for their two young children while B.J. was away for three years, writing regularly to him during all that time.

B.J. and Peg raised five children in all. The oldest, Judy, became a teacher and Candia farmer. A second daughter, Mary, was also a teacher and a third, Peggy, became a nurse and an attorney. Their oldest son, John, went to Virginia Military Institute and was a U.S. Navy pilot and then a commercial airline captain. The younger son became a newspaperman like his father and was briefly embedded with U.S. combat forces in Afghanistan.

His sometime companion Marcel Wallenstein of the Kansas newspaper once described B.J. to his readers as a man with a "ruddy face and smoldering blue eyes." He also hinted at B.J.'s sometimes prickly personality in one piece.

Yesterday McQuaid came out of nowhere and asked, "Who's riding in your jeep?"

"Nice people," I said. "They never give me an argument; they always do exactly as I say."

"I thought so," he sneered. "You look as if you'd gone soft – what about us riding together?"

WAR FRONTS HOME FIRES

"You mean nobody else will have you?" I said.

"I mean it would be a shame to spoil two jeeps," McQuaid answered. "If you'll get out early enough tomorrow morning I'll take you to a certain corps where they have a wonderful early morning briefing. But you must get out of the sack in the dark to be there on time."

Wallenstein knew what was good for him. He rode with B.J. that day.

Along with the stories and letters, I found notes of commendation in B.J.'s war trunk; both personal and official, from various U.S. Navy and Army officers high and low in the Pacific and European theaters. My father was considered a "good shipmate" by Naval commanders and a good comrade by Army officers.

"Soldier," read one handwritten note, unsigned on the back of an envelope, "Take care of this man. He's a liar in certain respects but one of the grandest people I've ever known."

THE VILLAGE OF COMBLANCHIEN

On Sept. 20, 1944, B.J. stopped at the small French village of Comblanchien. At first, he didn't know it was a village. Only a few houses were visible from the road as he and his driver roared down a deserted highway at 50 mph. But he noticed the peculiar circumstance that each of the half-dozen houses was gutted, as if by fire, and that one bore on the surface of its scorched and windowless wall some crude lettering, which seemed to have been splashed on hurriedly in black paint.

…We turned back and went to study the black paint legend. It read Vive Comblanchien! Vive La France! Vive Degaulle! A blonde teenage boy and a middle-aged woman appeared from behind the charred buildings.

As I questioned the boy and his mother about the significance of the painted lettering, a handful of additional citizens gathered beside the jeep.

They were nearly the whole population, now, of unlucky Comblanchien —three old ladies and an old man, a little girl, and a stocky chap about 40 who forthwith began stripping off his undershirt to display for our benefit horrible livid soars and burns which completely covered the upper portion of his body and were by no means fully healed.

These people told us the story of Comblanchien. It was what you would expect. At 10 o'clock at night on August 21, a force of several hundred Germans rolled into the village in a troop train. Leaving the train on the tracks, which cross through open fields just east of the village, they stormed into the public square and routed citizens from adjacent houses from their beds. They accused villagers of having given aid and shelter to bands of Maqui which had been active in the area.

The blond youth, who proudly announced that he had that morning enlisted in the French army at Dijon, agreed the Maqui had been active in the vicinity but denied Comblanchien had given them any more help than they were accustomed to get from all other communities in the region.

Germans, the people said, dragged 12 townsmen out of their beds and murdered them with machine guns. They seized 12 more citizens whom they took away with them as hostages. But before leaving they methodically set fire to almost every home, place of business, and public structure in the town, including the ancient church. The man who carried the scars said he was burned in his bed, not having been awakened by the noise of the shootings. He added however that as far as he knew no citizen had actually been burned to death in the fire.

Though Germans left the town blazing fiercely, the citizens rallied and managed to quell the flames but not until after most of the homes were rendered uninhabitable.

There were a handful of others besides themselves, people said, who had made the shift to live on in the village but most inhabitants had been forced to take shelter in neighboring communities.

The recital of this tragedy had taken perhaps 10 minutes. To investigate and adequately to report its overtones of human misery and social dislocation would take a year. But when covering war in a jeep, you do it in 10 minutes. You mutter inanities in pidgin French like "tres tragique" and "l'allemagnes and sauvages, vrainment" and the survivors of this savagery nod solemnly and solemnly shake hands all around – the little girl looking especially grave – and as you drive off in your jeep you cry Vive La France! And the people cry Vive L'Amerique!

As we rounded a bend of roadside trees we got a good closeup of the village in all its devastation. Afterward we never stopped to inquire when we saw other hamlets and even lonely isolated farmhouses in charred ruins – and there are many such sights south of Dijohn.

To certain criticisms of FFI for allegedly "terroristic tactics" against the retreating Germans – including reports of occasional summary executions of prisoners who have been implicated in some of these monstrosities – we were able to lend only half an ear.

WORKS CONSULTED

Garfield, Brian. *The Thousand Mile War*. Fairbanks: University of Alaska Press, 1969.

Huston, John. *An Open Book*. New York: Alfred A. Knopf, 1980.

Larson, Donald J. *Lucky's Life: Letters Home from Lt. William R. Larson, USNR, a Beloved, Son, Brother, and WWII Torpedo Bomber Fighter Pilot – Squadron VC 38*. United States: Donald J. Larson, 2016.

Lovelace, Alexander G. *The Media Offensive: How the Press and Public Opinion Shaped Allied Strategy During World War II*. Lawrence: University Press of Kansas, 2022.

Moseley, Ray. *Reporting War: How Foreign Correspondents Risked Capture, Torture and Death to Cover World War II*. New Haven: Yale University Press, 2017.

Polmar, Norman, and Allen, Thomas B. *World War II: The Encyclopedia of the War Years*. New York: Random House, 1991.

Sherrod, Robert. *Tarawa: The Story of a Battle*. Fredericksburg, TX: Admiral Nimitz Foundation, 1993.

White, Osmar. *Conquerors' Road*. Cambridge: Cambridge University Press, 1996.

Printed in the USA
CPSIA information can be obtained
at www.ICGtesting.com
LVHW091248170923
758435LV00003B/425